ST. LOUIS CARDINALS
TRIVIA TEASERS

RICHARD PENNINGTON

QUIZ MASTER BOOKS
Madison, Wisconsin

Library of Congress Control Number: 2008926370
ISBN: 978-1-934553-08-4

Editor: Mark Knickelbine
Book design: Rebecca Finkel
Photos: National Baseball Hall of Fame Library,
Cooperstown, New York

Printed in the United States of America.
13 12 11 10 09 08   6 5 4 3 2 1

Quiz Master Books, a division of Big Earth Publishing
923 Williamson Street • Madison, WI 53703
(800) 258-5830 • www.trailsbooks.com

TABLE OF

CONTENTS

Sportsman's Park, where baseball was played for almost a century—
from 1867 to 1965.

CHAPTER ONE

BEFORE
THE CARDINALS

The first professional baseball club to represent St. Louis was the Brown Stockings, owned by John R. Lucas. The team was part of the National Association in 1875, the final year for that league. They competed against such teams as the Keokuk Westerns, Philadelphia Centennials, Brooklyn Athletics, and Hartford Dark Blues. The dominant team in the NA was the Boston Red Stockings, who won the league's last four championships.

The NA folded due to a lack of central authority, too many franchises in small towns, and the suspected influence of gamblers. So six NA clubs (Boston, Hartford, New York, Philadelphia, Chicago, and St. Louis) and two independents (Louisville and Cincinnati) joined forces to establish the National League of Professional Base Ball Clubs, known more succinctly as the National League.

The Brown Stockings, managed by George McManus, played their games at Grand Avenue Ball Grounds, later the site of Sportsman's Park. This is where, on July 15, 1876, George Bradley of St. Louis pitched the first no-hitter in major league history, against Hartford. Bradley's record that year consisted of 45 wins and 19 losses. After the 1877 season, the Brown Stockings became embroiled in a game-fixing scandal that resulted in the expulsion of some players, and the demise of the franchise and that of the Louisville Grays. But just a few years later, a new baseball club in St. Louis took up the Brown Stockings' colors and nickname. The new Brown Stockings, soon called the Browns, were charter members of the American Association in 1882 and survive today as the St. Louis Cardinals. The 1882 club, owned by Chris von der Ahe and managed by Ned Cuthbert (who had stolen the first base in the game's history in 1863 while playing for the Philadelphia Keystones), posted a 37-43 record and finished in fifth place.

During its ten years of existence, the AA tried to challenge the more-established National League by offering its patrons cheaper ticket prices and easier access to libations. Since many of its backers were distilleries and breweries, it came to be known as the "Beer and Whiskey League." The AA and NL put on an early version of the World Series between 1882 and 1888. The St. Louis Browns represented the upstart league four times, coming away with the 1886 championship by defeating the Chicago White Stockings (now the Cubs), four games to two.

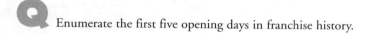

Enumerate the first five opening days in franchise history.

The first was on May 2, 1882, a 9-7 defeat of the Louisville Eclipse; the second was on May 15, 1883, a 7-4 defeat of the Cincinnati Red Stockings; the third was on May 1, 1884, a 4-2 defeat of the Indianapolis Blues; the fourth was on April 18, 1885, a 7-0 loss to the Pittsburgh Alleghenys; the fifth was on April 18, 1886, a 4-1 defeat of the Alleghenys.

Q In 1885, von der Ahe did something that drew the mockery of fans and sportswriters. What was it?

A He erected a larger-than-life statue of himself outside of Sportsman's Park. Years after he had lost his wealth and was reduced to tending bar in a small saloon, von der Ahe sometimes got a little help from Charles Comiskey, his former first baseman and manager (and future owner of the Chicago White Sox). In 1913, he died of cirrhosis of the liver and was buried in St. Louis' Bellefontaine Cemetery. The statue that formerly stood in front of Sportsman's Park adorns von der Ahe's grave.

Q This Connecticut native began his major league career in 1880 with the Troy Trojans, later moving downstate to the New York Gothams. Due to his size (6' 3", 220 pounds), they changed their name to the Giants. Who was he?

A Roger Connor, a member of the St. Louis club for four seasons. Connor, who had a none-too-impressive 8-37 mark as the team's manager in 1896, was baseball's home run king until Babe Ruth came along; not until 1921 did the Bambino surpass his career mark of 138. In 1976, the Veterans Committee sent the long-deceased Connor to Cooperstown.

Q Von der Ahe briefly owned a major league team in Cincinnati. What was it?

A The Cincinnati Porkers of the American Association. They were also known as the Kellys, after their catcher and manager, Michael "King" Kelly. He did not exactly rule with an iron fist, having the players choose their positions on a daily basis and letting them drink up after games. The Porkers had a 43-57 record late in the 1891 season when von der Ahe took a $12,000 offer from the cross-town Cincinnati Reds and folded the team.

Q When the American Association dissolved in 1891, the St. Louis Brown Stockings were one of four teams that merged into the National League. How did they do that first year?

A The season was split in half, but that seemed to make little difference. The Brown Stockings were 31-42 in the first half and 25-52 in the second half; they finished 46 games behind Boston.

Q St. Louis had five managers that year. Who were they?

A Jack Glasscock, Cub Stricker, Jack Crooks, George Gore, and Bob Caruthers.

Q A lot of sports history took place at the northeast corner of Grand Boulevard and Dodier Street on the north side of St. Louis. What was there?

A Amateur baseball games were played at that site as early as 1867. The owner, August Solari, called it Grand Avenue Ball Grounds. At first, it had a fenced field and a small grandstand with room for 800 fans. When the Brown Stockings took up residence there in 1875, Solari renamed the facility Sportsman's Park. It was put to other uses (such as cycling and shooting matches) for the four years after the original team folded and the new one arose in 1882. That American Association club used it for 12 years, which after time owner Chris von der Ahe moved out of Sportsman's Park. He built a little wooden stadium a few blocks northwest, at the intersection of Vandeventer and Natural Bridge avenues. This is where the National League club played from 1893 until the middle of the 1920 season. Von der Ahe called it New Sportsman's Park, although it would be outlived by the "old" one by some 4½ decades. When the Robison brothers, Frank and Stanley, bought the team from von der Ahe in 1899, they renamed it League Park. This facility, featuring an amusement park just beyond left field, later went by the name Robison Field. The Cardinals abandoned it and returned to Sportsman's Park in 1920, but as tenants of the American League Browns.

Q Why did the Cardinals return to their old home?

A It had been expanded and renovated into a steel-and-concrete structure with room for 18,000 fans. The Cards' new owner, Sam Breadon, convinced his Browns counterpart, Philip Ball, to allow his team to cohabit Sportsman's Park. The money Breadon got from the sale of Robison Field was used wisely by Branch Rickey, his manager and GM. He applied it to building a minor league system that would soon produce players who brought a lot of victories and glory to the St. Louis Cardinals. That farm system would later be copied by the other 15 big league franchises.

Q The last five of his 361 wins came with the St. Louis Brown Stockings in 1892. Name this St. Louis native.

A James "Pud" Galvin, who threw 5,941.1 innings—most of them with the Buffalo Bisons and Pittsburgh Alleghenys/Pirates.

Q How bad were the St. Louis Brown Stockings in 1897?

A They finished with a 23-102 record—12th in the 12-team National League and 20 games behind the 11th-place Louisville Colonels.

Q The St. Louis club was called the Perfectos for one season—1899. How did they do?

A They were not perfect, but they had by far the best season yet in franchise history. The Perfectos, managed by Patsy Tebeau, went 84-67 (a .556 mark that would not be topped until 1921) and drew 373,909 fans, almost double the previous record.

Q Name the outfielder for the 1899 team who collected 194 base hits—a rookie record until Albert Pujols came along.

A Emmett "Snags" Heidrick.

Q Who held down the shortstop position for the Perfectos/ Cardinals, the Browns, and then the Cards again between 1899 and 1918?

A Bobby Wallace, who also managed the Browns in 1911 and 1912.

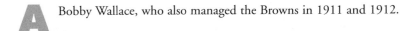

Q How did the team come to be called the Cardinals?

A They had adopted a new red color scheme in 1900. The oft-told story is that *St. Louis Republic* sportswriter Willie McHale overheard a female fan remark, "What a lovely shade of cardinal." He began using it in his column, and the name was soon adopted by one and all. Only later did the name come to be associated with a bird.

Q This catcher was coming to the end of his 17-year career when he played 60 games with the 1900 St. Louis club, batting .248 and driving in 28 runs. Who was he?

A Wilbert Robinson, who would go on to manage Brooklyn from 1914 to 1931. Uncle Robbie's teams won 1,375 games.

Q Robinson had a teammate on the 1900 St. Louis team who would have an even longer and far more successful managing career. Who was he?

A Third baseman John McGraw, a.k.a. "Little Napoleon," who managed the New York Giants from 1902 until 1932, winning 10 pennants and three championships along the way. When he died in 1934, his belongings included a list of all the black players he wanted to sign but could not.

Q What Irish-born outfielder managed St. Louis from 1901 to 1903?

A Patsy Donovan, who had a .300 batting average with a variety of teams—primarily Pittsburgh. He managed the Pirates, as well as the Cardinals, Washington Senators, Brooklyn Superbas, and Boston Red Sox. It was during his stint with the Cards that Donovan broke Sam Thompson's career major league record of 1,401 games in right field. That record would not last long, as Willie Keeler passed him in 1906. Much later, Donovan ran the baseball program at Phillips Academy in Massachusetts, where one of his players was George H.W. Bush, the 41st president of the United States.

Q Who holds the team record for most singles in a season?

A In 1901, left-handed Jesse Burkett—en route to a .382 batting average—had 180 singles out of a league-leading 228 hits. The West Virginia native was a clever bunter and had the speed to leg out many infield hits. Burkett twice batted over .400 for the Cleveland Spiders before coming to St. Louis. Known as "the Crab" because of his caustic barbs and never-ending complaints, he treated rivals, fans, and teammates with equal venom.

Q The Cardinals got some bad news in 1902. What was it?

A The Milwaukee Brewers of the fledgling American League moved to St. Louis. Furthermore, they took the Cards' old name and became the St. Louis Browns, and had the unmitigated gall to lure away several of the team's best players—Jesse Burkett, shortstop Bobby Wallace, and three top pitchers. As if that were not enough, the Browns shared Sportsman's Park with the Cardinals.

Q Were the Browns serious competition for the Cardinals?

A Be it ever so humble, there is no place like home. And home was often last place for the Brownies. They finished in the AL cellar 10 times from 1902 to 1953, when they moved to Baltimore and became the Orioles. The Browns put together just 11 winning seasons and lost more than 100 games eight times. They would win the AL pennant in 1944, when major league baseball was largely depleted because of World War II. Bad as they were, the Browns generally had better attendance than the Cards in the early years of the century.

Q This New York Giants rookie got his 17-year career off to a nice start on September 14, 1903, by throwing a five-inning (the game was called due to an impending storm) no-hitter against the Cardinals. Who was he?

A Leon "Red" Ames, a member of the St. Louis staff from 1915 to 1919. During that time, he led the NL in saves and relief wins once each.

Q What pitcher holds the team record for most complete games in a season?

A Jack Taylor, who completed 39 games in 1904. This Ohio native debuted with the Cubs in 1898 and was traded to St. Louis in return for Mordecai Brown. Taylor was really quite an iron man, throwing 187 straight complete games between June 1901 and August 1906, along with 15 relief appearances. He was with the Cubs when they won the 1907 World Series.

Q A century after he retired, he still holds the major league record for most games played at first base—2,377 between 1888 and 1907. Who was he?

A Jake Beckley, a Cardinal the last four years of his career. His batting average was north of .300 13 times, and he stole 315 bases.

Q A player-manager with the Cardinals in 1904 and 1905, he had already won a lot of fame with the Boston Beaneaters. Identify this native of Madison, Wisconsin.

A Charles "Kid" Nichols, who amassed 361 victories over a 15-year big league career. Admired for his smooth delivery and steadfast consistency, Nichols was the youngest man to have reached the 300-win plateau, having done it at age 30. His salary in 1898 was $2,400, highest in the National League. Nichols' numbers would have been even greater, but for two seasons he chose to pitch for a Kansas City minor league team he had bought and for whom he won 48 games. His managerial record with the Cards consisted of two teams that finished in fifth and sixth place. Nichols spent his final two seasons with the Phillies.

Q After having three managers in 1905, St. Louis settled on one man for the next three seasons. Who was he?

A John McCloskey, under whom the team went from bad to worse—losing 98 games, then 101, then 105. McCloskey is best remembered for having organized the Texas League at a meeting in Austin in 1887.

Q Who holds the team record for most innings pitched in a season?

A Grant "Stoney" McGlynn, who was on the mound for 352.1 innings in 1907. That mark led the National League, as did his 112 walks and 329 hits surrendered.

Q The 1908 Cardinals went a woeful 49-105, with three regulars batting below .200. Who was their top hitter that year?

A Outfielder Red Murray, who batted .282, hit seven home runs, and drove in 62 runs. Life got a lot better for this Pennsylvania native, however. The next year, he joined the New York Giants and played in three straight World Series.

Q The Cardinals bought him after he threw a no-hitter for Shreveport of the Texas League early in 1909. Later in the season he hurled a 16-inning victory against the Phillies. Identify him.

A Bob Harmon. Two years later, he had a career-best 23-16 record as St. Louis posted just its third winning season. The 41 games Harmon started in 1911 remains a club record.

Q What highly skilled first baseman, a native of La Crosse, Wisconsin, played for the Cardinals from 1907 to 1913? Hint: He was known as "Big Ed" and "the Candy Kid."

A Ed Konetchy, who also spent time with the Pittsburgh Pirates, Pittsburgh Rebels of the Federal League, Boston Braves, Brooklyn Robins, and Philadelphia Phillies. Konetchy was a bright spot on an otherwise poor Cardinals team. He stole 25 bases in 1909, had a 20-game hitting streak in 1910, and drove in 88 runs in 1911.

Q What scrawny second baseman was traded from Cincinnati to St. Louis in 1910?

A Miller Huggins. The Mighty Mite was a switch-hitter and an excellent leadoff man. He was also sure-handed in the field. Huggins was the Cards' player-manager by 1913 and had retired to the bench four years later. The best he could do was a couple of third-place finishes.

Q Huggins had a law degree and was a shrewd investor, so he had accumulated some money. What did he try to do with it?

A He sought to buy the Cardinals. When his offer was turned down after the 1917 season, Huggins quit. Soon thereafter, American League president Ban Johnson urged Yankees owner Jacob Ruppert to sign him—in spite of a rather undistinguished record. That changed quickly as he established himself as the boss of what had been an unruly bunch of carousers and bad actors (with the exception of the saintly Lou Gehrig). New York won six AL pennants and three World Series with Huggins at the helm.

Q Identify "the Duke of Tralee."

A That was the nickname of pugnacious Roger Bresnahan, who was tough on teammates, opponents, umpires, and owners. Noisy confrontations were the norm for this brawling Irishman. He was primarily a catcher, but he could play any position. He even started nine games as a pitcher and was said to have a dazzling repertoire. Christy Mathewson's battery mate with the New York Giants early in the 20th century, Bresnahan defied the taunts of other players by coming up with head and thigh-protection gear. Other catchers soon were doing the same. He played for and managed the Cardinals from 1909 to 1912, but they never rose above fifth place in the NL.

Q This outfielder showed a lot of promise, but his clowning antics angered the New York Giants management, so he was shipped to St. Louis after just two games in 1908. Name him.

A Steve Evans, who had an unusual knack for being hit by pitches. He was plunked 31 times in 1910, which stood as a major league record for 61 years and remains the Cards' record. In one game against Brooklyn, Evans was hit three times.

Q The Cards were relatively successful in 1911, going 75-74 and drawing a record 447,768 fans. What did Mrs. Schuyler Britton, the team owner, do in response?

A She rewarded player-manager Roger Bresnahan with a five-year contract at $10,000 per year. But they lost 12 more games the next year, and attendance dropped almost by half. Britton, as owners are wont to do, second-guessed her manager publicly. When Bresnahan responded with some choice dugout repartee, he was fired forthwith. He played three more years with the Cubs, all while engaged in a legal battle with Britton, finally winning a $20,000 settlement.

Q In early July 1911, the Cardinals were on a train going from Philadelphia to Boston. What happened on that trip to the Hub City?

A There was a serious accident in which 12 people were killed and 47 injured. Since the Cardinals were riding toward the rear of the train, none of them were seriously hurt. In fact, led by Roger Bresnahan and Ed Konetchy, they took part in the rescue effort, carrying many passengers to safety. St. Louis was three games out of first place when the accident happened but faded to a distant fifth.

Q This native of Austin, Texas, spent six seasons in Pittsburgh and three in St. Louis. In 1912 while with the Bucs, he set a record that endures today—36 triples. Who was he?

A Outfielder Owen "Chief" Wilson.

Q The Pirates and Cards had an eight-player swap on December 12, 1913. Who was involved?

A Those coming to St. Louis were second baseman Dots Miller, pitcher Hank Robinson, third baseman Cozy Dolan, utility infielder Art Butler, and outfielder Owen Wilson. In return, Pittsburgh got pitcher Bob Harmon, third baseman Mike Mowrey, and first baseman Ed Konetchy. The Cards had the better end of the deal, which attested to the trading acumen of manager Miller Huggins.

Second baseman Rogers Hornsby, one of the all-time greats.
He also managed the Cardinals, Giants, Braves, Cubs, Browns, and Reds.

CHAPTER TWO

RAJAH

R ogers Hornsby, a 5' 11", 175-pound Texan, was the greatest right-handed batter in the history of the game. Hornsby was imperturbable at the plate, never arguing with umpires, never being tossed from a game in a playing career that began in 1915 and concluded in 1937. He hit line drives all over the field, had speed that would later draw comparisons with Mickey Mantle, and was a splendid second baseman, with a .957 career fielding average.

Hornsby, known as "Rajah" to those who those who loved him as well as those who feared him, did some things that are unlikely to ever be duplicated. He holds the modern record for highest batting average in a season, .424 in 1924, and he won the Triple Crown in 1922 and 1925. He was the National League's MVP twice, although the award was not instituted until he had been playing for nine years. Hornsby led the league in batting every year from 1920 to 1925, averaging an unfathomable .402. He had lots of power too, hitting 301 home runs. Hornsby, who had a 33-game hitting streak in 1922 (when he became the only man in baseball history to hit over .400 and stroke more than 40 home runs), ended up with a .358 lifetime average—second only to Ty Cobb. He feared no pitcher, since he could hit them all.

In the middle of the 1925 season, owner Sam Breadon decided to move manager Branch Rickey upstairs and replace him with Hornsby. The next year, the franchise came of age as the Cardinals drew a record 681,575 fans and beat the New York Yankees in the

World Series. When Babe Ruth made an ill-advised stolen-base attempt in the ninth inning of Game 7, Hornsby made the tag to end the Series.

Handsome, forthright, and quite popular with the fans, Hornsby could nevertheless be a difficult person to handle. He was a member of the Ku Klux Klan, he gambled compulsively on the ponies, and he had a barbed-wire personality. Owners and GMs often got Hornsby at his most belligerent. He had no qualms about telling them to get out of his clubhouse, mind their own business, and let him do his job. Breadon received plenty of verbal abuse from Hornsby, and a contract dispute brought matters to a head. It mattered not that the team had just won the World Series and that Hornsby was at the height of his popularity. Breadon sent him to the New York Giants in exchange for second baseman Frankie Frisch and pitcher Jimmy Ring. Hornsby later managed the Giants, Braves, Cubs, Browns, and Reds, although his final moment of baseball glory was in 1929 when Chicago won the NL pennant. Hornsby batted what was for him a pedestrian .380 and led the league in runs scored.

Who went 12-23 and made a league-high 51 appearances for the 1916 Cardinals?

Lee Meadows, who pitched for the Cards, Phillies, and Pirates in a 15-year career. He helped Pittsburgh reach the 1925 and 1927 World Series, starting—and losing—the opening game both times.

Q Who was Sam Breadon, and where had he come from?

A This man, a native of New York, moved to St. Louis right around the turn of the century, making his fortune with several automobile dealerships. He invested a modest $2,000 in the Cardinals in 1917 when they were a perennial doormat. Three years later, he put in $350,000 to become the team's majority owner and president. Under his watch, they rose to be one of the premier teams in all of baseball.

Q In 1920, the major leagues outlawed the spitball. But 17 men were "grandfathered," being allowed to keep throwing wet ones for the remainder of their careers. Two played for St. Louis. Name them and the others.

A Marv Goodwin and Bill Doak are the men in question, along with Red Faber (White Sox), Doc Ayers and Dutch Leonard (Tigers), Ray "Slim" Caldwell and Stan Coveleski (Indians), Phil Douglas (Giants), Dana Fillingim (Braves), Ray Fisher (Reds), Burleigh Grimes and Clarence Mitchell (Dodgers), Jack Quinn (Yankees), Dick Rudolph (Braves), Allan Russell (Red Sox), and Urban Shocker and Allen Sothoron (Browns).

Q This superb left fielder was just coming into his own in 1921, when he batted .350 (third best in the NL), hit 17 homers, and drove in 102 runs. But he only played 62 games in '22 and was diagnosed with a brain tumor. By November, he was dead. Identify this native of Wrightsville, Ohio.

A Austin McHenry.

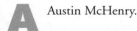

Q Outfielder Cliff Heathcote was involved in a unique trade on May 30, 1922. Of what did it consist?

A Branch Rickey traded him for the Cubs' Max Flack between games of a St. Louis–Chicago doubleheader. He and Flack switched uniforms between morning and afternoon games, both of which the Cubs won. Later that season, Heathcote was 5-for-5 with four RBIs and five runs scored in Chicago's 26-23 defeat of the Phillies.

Q The St. Louis Browns nearly won the 1922 American League pennant. So what was the bold prediction of Browns' owner Philip Ball?

A He stated that Sportsman's Park would soon be the site of a World Series. In anticipation, he boosted its seating capacity from 18,000 to 30,000. Ball turned out to be right—there was a World Series in Sportsman's Park in 1926, but the host team was the Cardinals and not the Browns.

Q The Cardinals and Browns had company at Sportsman's Park in 1923. Who were the interlopers?

A The St. Louis All-Stars of the National Football League. Ollie Kraehe, owner, manager, promoter, coach, and part-time player, wore enough hats to fill a small checkroom. His All-Stars, who played some games at the stadium before as few as 719 souls, went 1-4-2 that year and folded.

Q When was the first time a St. Louis pitcher threw a no-hitter?

A On July 17, 1924, fastballer Jesse Haines did it against the Boston Braves. He had pitched briefly for the Cincinnati Reds in 1918 but found a place in the Cardinals' starting rotation two years later. Haines, who learned the knuckleball and thus was able to play until age 44, took part in four World Series. He was inducted into the Hall of Fame in 1970, but not without some quiet grumbling. His career stats were good, but not truly great: a 210-158 record, 3.64 ERA, and 3,208 innings pitched. Some observers thought he got in because of the presence of teammates and contemporaries on the Veterans Committee.

Q Rickey was promoted to general manager during the 1925 season. Breadon gave him wide-ranging authority—with one major exception. What was it?

A The owner reserved the right to choose the Cards' manager.

Q The Cards and Phillies played a doubleheader at the Baker Bowl on September 16, 1926. Who prevailed?

A St. Louis won both games, the first of which was a 23-3 rout. The Cardinals scored a team-record 12 runs in the third inning.

Q He was one of the game's best pitchers and probably its most renowned alcoholic. His constant drunkenness and insubordination led the Cubs to sell him to St. Louis for the waiver price early in the 1926 season, but he proved he could still pitch. Name this native of Elba, Nebraska.

A Grover Cleveland Alexander. He was the hero of the '26 World Series, with two complete-game victories and a save in Game 7 (although he had been out drinking the night before).

Q Alexander had one more great season left—1927, when he went 21-10. But how did he acquit himself in the 1928 World Series against the Yankees?

A He started Game 2, pitched 5 innings, and gave up 10 hits. Alexander's ERA for that Series was 19.80.

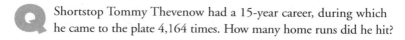

Q Shortstop Tommy Thevenow had a 15-year career, during which he came to the plate 4,164 times. How many home runs did he hit?

A Two, both of them of the inside-the-park variety, in 1926. He went 10-for-24 in that year's World Series. Thevenow later spent time with the Phillies, Pirates, Reds, and Braves.

Q After Game 2 of the 1926 World Series, the teams rode the rails from New York to St. Louis. What did Mayor Victor J. Miller do to celebrate the Cards' arrival?

A He was part of a large crowd that gathered to welcome the team at Union Station. Miller stood at a podium and presented Rogers Hornsby with a new Lincoln sedan, which had been paid for by some of the city's top businessmen. Other members of the team received a new hat, a new pair of shoes, and an engraved white-gold watch.

Q What did each member of the St. Louis club get for winning the 1926 World Series?

A $5,584.51, while the Yanks were given $3,417.75 each.

Q What St. Louis players have the fewest and most strikeouts in a season?

A In 1927, Frankie Frisch had 617 at-bats and whiffed just 10 times. By contrast, Jim Edmonds came to the plate 525 times in 2000 and had 167 strikeouts.

Q In the 1925 World Series, Pittsburgh beat Washington in seven games. The Pirates' manager moved to St. Louis in 1928 and got the Cards into the Series, although they fell to the Yanks. Name him.

A Bill McKechnie, who won another title with the 1940 Cincinnati Reds. McKechnie was not a typical manager for that era. He sang in the church choir (thus his nickname of "the Deacon"), and did not smoke, drink, or curse.

Q The New York Yankees had swept the Pirates in the 1927 World Series. How would they fare the next year against the Cardinals?

A They won all four games convincingly. Babe Ruth was 10-for-16 at the plate as New York demolished St. Louis by a combined score of 27 to 10. As he had done in 1926, Ruth blasted three home runs over the right field pavilion at Sportsman's Park in Game 4, serving as a punctuation mark on the Yankees' dominance. Lou Gehrig also had an outstanding Series, driving in nine runs.

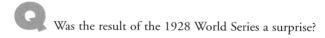

Q Was the result of the 1928 World Series a surprise?

A Somewhat. The Cardinals really were a powerful club, having gone from 89 wins in 1926, to 92 wins in 1927, to 95 wins in 1928. The defending champion Yankees had won their third straight pennant but had a depleted lineup. Pitcher Herb Pennock sat out the Series with a sore arm. Center fielder Earle Combs had a broken finger and was available only as a pinch-hitter. Second baseman Tony Lazzeri had an injured arm, and Babe Ruth was playing on a bum ankle. But the Bambino and the Iron Horse abused the St. Louis pitching staff with reckless abandon.

Q The Cards had lost 12 straight games going into the second half of a doubleheader in Philadelphia on July 6, 1929. How did they do against Connie Mack's club?

A They won, 28-6. That remains the most runs scored in a game in franchise history.

By 1930, it was clear that the "dead ball" era was over. In fact, some fans wondered whether the ball had been juiced a bit too much. Give an example.

Six National League clubs had batting averages above .300, led by the Giants (.319), Phillies (.315), and Cardinals (.314). Ironically, batting in that year's World Series was anemic. Philadelphia hit a meager .197, and St. Louis was little better at .200. But 18 of the Athletics' 35 hits went for extra bases. Perhaps the lack of offense was a testament to the solid pitching on both sides. George Earnshaw (Series MVP) won two games for the Phillies and had a 0.72 ERA in 25 innings of mound work. Lefty Grove was not far behind, winning two with a 1.42 ERA in 19 innings.

In the late 1920s and early 1930s, the Philadelphia Athletics established themselves as one of the elite teams in major league baseball. It appeared that the "Mackmen" had displaced the New York Yankees as kings of the American League, but all of this proved to be a temporary phenomenon. They met the Cardinals in the 1931 World Series. Did they three-peat?

No, Philly lost in seven games. Forty years would pass before the A's again reached the postseason, by which time they were in Oakland (with a 13-season stretch in Kansas City). The '31 Series was a reversal of fortunes of what happened in 1930. The main newcomer on Gabby Street's team was 27-year-old rookie Pepper Martin, who batted .500, scored five runs, drove in five runs, stole five bases, and made a running catch to stifle Philadelphia's ninth-inning rally in Game 7.

Q What St. Louis pitcher won both starts and threw seven innings of no-hit ball in the 1931 Series?

A Burleigh Grimes, a native of Emerald, Wisconsin. He was among those pitchers who were given a waiver after the spitball was banned in 1920. Grimes used it to his advantage and to the consternation of opposing batters.

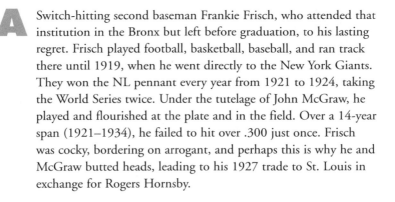

Q Who was the "Fordham Flash"?

A Switch-hitting second baseman Frankie Frisch, who attended that institution in the Bronx but left before graduation, to his lasting regret. Frisch played football, basketball, baseball, and ran track there until 1919, when he went directly to the New York Giants. They won the NL pennant every year from 1921 to 1924, taking the World Series twice. Under the tutelage of John McGraw, he played and flourished at the plate and in the field. Over a 14-year span (1921–1934), he failed to hit over .300 just once. Frisch was cocky, bordering on arrogant, and perhaps this is why he and McGraw butted heads, leading to his 1927 trade to St. Louis in exchange for Rogers Hornsby.

Frisch, National League MVP in 1931, was a manager, too. Was he successful in that endeavor?

His first full year as the Cards' manager was in 1934, and we know they won the championship. But their fortunes gradually declined over the next five years, as did attendance. Frisch had retired as a player after the 1937 season, but he was replaced the next year with Mike Gonzalez. He managed the Pittsburgh Pirates (1940–1946) and the Chicago Cubs (1949–1951) but never again reached the postseason.

Who was known as "Old Sarge"?

Gabby Street, a second-team catcher from 1904 to 1912 with the Reds, Braves, Senators, and Highlanders (Yankees). The Alabama native took over as manager of the Cards late in the 1929 season and won a pair of pennants and one World Series before they faltered in 1932. He also spent one season with the bottom-feeding Browns. They won just 53 games under Street's guidance before he was given a pink slip.

Q Street's 1930 Cardinals won 92 games and took the NL pennant. Were they the only winner in St. Louis that year?

A No. The St. Louis Stars went 69-29 and beat the Detroit Stars in a playoff to win the Negro National League championship.

Q This Cardinals southpaw led the NL in both strikeouts and walks in 1930 and '31. Who was he?

A "Wild" Bill Hallahan, so named not because of his temperament, but because he sometimes had trouble finding the strike zone. Hallahan, star of the St. Louis staff before Dizzy Dean arrived, was at his best in the postseason. In seven World Series games, he pitched 39.2 innings, winning three games and losing one, with an ERA of 1.51.

Q Flint Rhem was due to start for the Cardinals against the Dodgers at Ebbets Field on September 17, 1930. What prevented him from taking the mound?

A Rhem was missing for 24 hours before he showed up at the Cards' hotel with an unlikely alibi. He claimed to have been kidnapped by gamblers, taken to New Jersey, and forced to imbibe bootleg whiskey. Years later, he confessed it was all a lie.

Q How many statistical leaders did the St. Louis pitchers have in the 1930 season?

A Only two: Hi Bell led the league with eight saves, and Bill Hallahan had 177 strikeouts.

Q The 1931 Cardinals won the World Series and drew 623,960 fans to Sportsman's Park. How did they do at the gate the next year, after going 72-82 and finishing in sixth place?

A Attendance dropped by more than half, to 290,370. Many major league teams drew fewer fans as the Great Depression worsened, and St. Louis was no different.

Q He was a native of Berkeley, California, was part of two World Series championship teams with the Cardinals, and led the NL in batting in 1931 (.349). Identify him.

A Outfielder Charles "Chick" Hafey, a quiet man who was somewhat overshadowed by some of the more colorful individuals who played on the Cardinals of the late 1920s and early 1930s. Hafey's career faltered because of a sinus condition for which he had to wear glasses on the field—a rarity at the time.

Q Hafey, who got the first hit in the history of the All-Star Game (a second-inning single in 1933), is still part owner of a National League record. What is it?

A That of most consecutive at-bats with a base hit; he had 10 in July 1929. Hafey, who retired with a career batting average of .317, 164 home runs, and 833 RBIs, was inducted into the Hall of Fame in 1971, two years before his death.

Q What was the derivation of the term Gashouse Gang as it related to the St. Louis Cardinals of the early and mid-1930s?

A The Gashouse District, located on Manhattan's Lower East Side, housed several large gas tanks. It was a tough and foul-smelling neighborhood, full of vagrants and drunks. A group of these people, calling themselves the Gashouse Gang, often wandered the area, seeking ways to wreak havoc. This fact was known to New York sportswriters, who took the liberty to apply the name to the visiting Cardinals. They were supposed to have arrived in Grand Central Station one day, still wearing the dirty, rain-soaked uniforms they had worn the day before against the Boston Braves. The team lacked the luxury of extra uniforms, and even when they were clean they tended to be patched in two or three spots. Furthermore, many of the players did not shave before games, they favored chewing tobacco, they played schoolboy-style pranks, and they spoke with Southern accents, using improper grammar now and then. Even so, they captured the imagination of baseball fans all over the country. They were a clear contrast to the high-and-mighty Yankees.

Q What players are best remembered as being part of the Gashouse Gang?

A The short list would have to include Leo Durocher, Dizzy Dean, Joe Medwick, Ripper Collins, and Pepper Martin.

Q This rough-and-tumble group was put together by the pious Branch Rickey, the team's general manager. How and why?

A Rickey had joined the Cardinals two decades earlier, when they were a marginal team teetering on bankruptcy, and had turned them into one of the National League's best. Rickey realized that a low-budget, small-city team could compete with those in New York and Chicago if it had a chain of minor league teams (and the Cards had more than 20 at one time) to find young players, train them, and send them to St. Louis when they were ready. All this could be done more cheaply than merely purchasing established players—the best example being Boston Red Sox owner Tom Yawkey, who time and again lavished big contracts on men who were past their primes.

Q In the mid-1930s, a reporter asked one Cardinals scout what kind of players he tended to look for. What was his response?

A "Hard guys. I don't care whether they can field or not. I want strong-armed, strong-legged guys who can hit, run, and throw. Guys like Pepper Martin."

Q Who was the "Wild Hoss of the Osage"?

A Outfielder and third baseman Pepper Martin, a native of Temple, Oklahoma. One of the most colorful and exciting players of his era, Martin was also a key member of the Cards' Gashouse Gang of the 1930s. After having spent seven years in St. Louis' deep farm system, he took over for centerfielder Taylor Douthit, who had been sent to the Reds. Martin proceeded to bat .300 as the Cardinals won the NL pennant and beat the A's in the 1931 World Series. In that seven-game Series, he went 12-for-24 and stole five bases. Three years later, it was more of the same, with the Cards winning the title (against Detroit) and Martin shining brightly on the biggest stage in baseball. He retired in 1944, having played his whole career with the Cardinals. Martin was a simple farm boy whose feet were fleet and whose bat was hot at just the right times. Rickey called him "one of nature's noblemen."

Q On August 26, 1949, Martin got in a little trouble. What was it?

A While managing a team in the Florida International League, he choked an umpire. For that indiscretion, Martin was fined $100 and suspended for the remainder of the season.

Q He won 43 games for St. Louis between 1932 and 1934, helped the Cubs win a pair of pennants, and had a no-hitter for Brooklyn in his final season. Identify him.

A James "Tex" Carleton.

Q This fireballing righthander out of Iowa led the National League in strikeouts seven straight years with the Dodgers. By the time he got to St. Louis in 1933, he was 41 years old with a tired arm. Name him.

A Clarence "Dazzy" Vance. He had a unique and fearsome style on the mound, with a high leg kick and a waggle of the foot before catapulting the ball toward home plate. Vance added a flamboyant touch by wearing a red undershirt with sliced sleeves that twirled into ribbons, which made his delivery that much more disconcerting.

Q Vance had won the 1924 NL most valuable player award when he had 28 wins, 262 strikeouts, and an ERA of 2.16. But it was a controversial decision. Why?

A The Cards' Rogers Hornsby had some staggering numbers of his own: .424 batting average, 227 hits, 43 doubles, and 121 runs— and he still walked 89 times. But one sportswriter, displeased by the Rajah's prickly personality, left him off his ballot entirely. Only because of this omission did Vance get the MVP trophy. Hornsby was actually pretty gracious about it and insisted that Vance was worthy.

Q This Arkansas native learned the basics of pitching while in the army and was playing for a semipro team in San Antonio when a Cardinals scout noticed him. Thus began the singular career of what man?

A Jay "Dizzy" Dean. He was a 21-year-old rookie in 1932 when he joined St. Louis, which was then coming off a World Series defeat of the A's. He won 18 games and led the league in strikeouts, shutouts, and innings pitched. Dean was an all-around baseball player—a superb fielder, a .258 batter, and a speedy baserunner. He manhandled batters from 1933 to 1936, winning 102 games. Although he was the ace of the Cardinals staff, Dean often pitched in relief between starts. In a 1933 game against Chicago, he struck out 17 batters, a major league record at the time.

Q How did Dean do in 1934?

A He was simply spectacular, going 30-7 and winning two games in the World Series. Dean was a runaway winner of the MVP award. Bold and given to making predictions and backing them up in full, he was a central figure of the Gashouse Gang.

Q What happened to Dizzy Dean in Game 4 of the 1934 World Series against Detroit at Sportsman's Park?

A Dean entered the game as a pinch runner and tried to break up a double play. But Billy Rogell's relay throw struck him in the head, knocking him unconscious. The Cardinals lost, and the Series was tied. The headline the next morning in the *St. Louis Post-Dispatch* read: "Dean's head x-rays show nothing." It was never completely clear whether Frisch sent Dean into the game or whether he just went out on his own. Dean was able to come back the next day and pitch, although he lost. Brother Paul Dean won Game 6, and Dizzy took Game 7 for the Cards.

Dean's upward trajectory ended in the 1937 All-Star Game in Washington. What happened?

 He was on the mound when Earl Averill of the Cleveland Indians hit a line drive that broke Dean's toe. He was out for a while, came back too soon, and changed his delivery in a way that favored his sore toe. As a result, Dean hurt his arm and lost his great fastball. By 1938, he was washed up, although the Cubs bought him for $185,000. Relying on guile, he helped them win the 1938 National League pennant and pitched in Game 2 of the World Series, falling to the New York Yankees. Even after retiring (he had a one-game comeback with the St. Louis Browns in 1947), Dean's popularity continued unabated due to his work as a radio and TV broadcaster. Malapropisms and blatant disregard of the rules of the English language were the norm for him, and fans did not seem to mind.

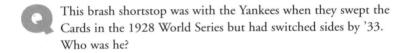

 This brash shortstop was with the Yankees when they swept the Cards in the 1928 World Series but had switched sides by '33. Who was he?

Leo Durocher, who would have a long and rather tumultuous career as a manager with the Dodgers, Giants, Cubs, and Astros. His finest moment undoubtedly came during Brooklyn's 1947 spring training, when he quashed a rebellion by players who were displeased by the impending integration of their team in the form of Jackie Robinson. A pro at the card table and at the horse track, Durocher is known for having uttered the phrase "nice guys finish last."

Q What muscular son of Hungarian immigrants occupied left field at Sportsman's Park for most of the 1930s? Hint: His nickname was "Ducky," but no one dared say that to his face.

A Joe Medwick, who later played with the Dodgers, Giants, and Braves. Commissioner Kenesaw Mountain Landis tossed Medwick out of Game 7 of the 1934 World Series after he hit a triple and went into third base a little too high and hard. This provoked Tigers fans to begin an aerial barrage of fruit, vegetables, bottles, and seat cushions. Medwick played for 17 seasons and was a ten-time All-Star with a .324 lifetime batting average. He was the NL's most valuable player in 1937, winning the Triple Crown.

Q In 1944, Medwick took part in a USO tour and was among a group of people given an audience with Pope Pius XII. What happened at that meeting in Rome?

A The Pope asked his vocation, to which Medwick replied, "Your Holiness, I'm Joe Medwick. I, too, used to be a Cardinal."

Q They called him "Daffy," but such a nickname did not reflect the personality of a rather quiet and serious man. Identify this native of Lucas, Arkansas.

A Paul Dean. Upon joining his brother Dizzy on St. Louis' pitching staff in 1934, the latter predicted, "Me and Paul will win 45 games." They did even better by winning 49 (30 by Dizzy, 19 by Paul). With such production, the Cards got to the World Series and the Deans won two games apiece to beat the Tigers. In 1935, his sophomore year, Paul Dean again won 19 for the Cardinals. But he soon hurt his arm and fell into mediocrity.

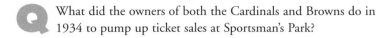 What did the owners of both the Cardinals and Browns do in 1934 to pump up ticket sales at Sportsman's Park?

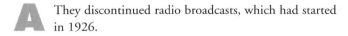 They discontinued radio broadcasts, which had started in 1926.

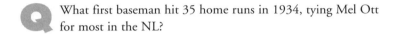 What first baseman hit 35 home runs in 1934, tying Mel Ott for most in the NL?

James Anthony "Ripper" Collins, who started all 154 regular season games for the Cards that year. He also had a career-best .333 batting average and 128 ribbies. A fun-maker off the field—like many of his Gashouse Gang teammates—but relentlessly serious on it, Collins later played for the Cubs and helped them reach the 1938 World Series.

St. Louis had dropped to sixth in the 1932 National League race and fifth in 1933 before resuming its place at the top in 1934, edging the defending champ Giants in the final three weeks of the season. Who would the Cardinals meet in the World Series?

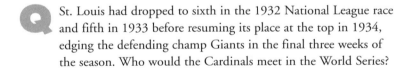 The Detroit Tigers, making their fourth appearance and still seeking their first title. It was the last time a World Series featured two player-managers—Frankie Frisch for the Cards and Mickey Cochrane for the Tigers.

Q The Cards and Tigers split their first two games at Navin Field, but Detroit took two of the next three back in St. Louis. Game 6 was close, a 4-3 Cardinals victory with Paul Dean (who had thrown a no-hitter against Brooklyn late in the season) getting the decision. What about Game 7?

A It was an 11-0 laugher for the Cardinals as they secured their third championship in nine years. Toward the end of that game, the indefatigable Dizzy Dean was having a bit too much fun on the mound. Frisch called time, walked over from second base, and told him, "If you don't stop clowning around, I'm going to take you out of the game." Dean ignored him and continued to pitch.

Q What happened at the Polo Grounds on Wednesday, August 14, 1935?

A What was then the largest midweek crowd in National League history (50,868) saw the Giants and Cardinals split a doubleheader. Carl Hubbell won the first for New York, while Bill Hallahan took the nightcap.

Q In a game against the Cubs on September 27, 1936, Johnny Mize was ejected. The rookie who took his place committed an error at first base and struck out in his only time up. He never got into another major league game—at least as a player. Who was the rook?

A Walter Alston. By 1954, he had been appointed as the Brooklyn Dodgers' manager. Alston won seven NL pennants (and four World Series) in his 23-year tenure as manager of the Brooklyn/LA team. By the time he retired in 1976, Alston had been on the bench for 3,658 games.

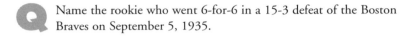

Q Name the rookie who went 6-for-6 in a 15-3 defeat of the Boston Braves on September 5, 1935.

A Terry Moore, a native of Vernon, Alabama, who never played for another team in his 11-year career. Moore, a centerfielder who could run and throw, may have been overshadowed by more colorful teammates, but he captained two of the Cardinals' World Series championship teams (1942 and 1946). After returning from the war, his batting declined somewhat and he fought injuries. In the 1950s, he served as a coach in St. Louis and managed the Phillies in the second half of the 1954 season.

Q In 1938, manager Frankie Frisch sent him up to pinch-hit 43 times, and he got 20 hits. Name this native of Coalinga, California.

A Frenchy Bordagaray, a gifted but erratic player. This is why he went from team to team (White Sox, Dodgers, Cardinals, Reds, Yankees, and Dodgers again). Bordagaray would be on a World Series winner with the '41 Yanks.

Q The Cardinals and Dodgers were playing the second game of a doubleheader at Ebbets Field on June 18, 1940, when a violent incident took place. Recount it.

A Joe Medwick, who had been traded from St. Louis to Brooklyn just six days earlier, was beaned by Cards pitcher Bob Bowman. This was allegedly in retaliation for third base coach Chuck Dressen stealing signs; the two had also quarreled the night before in a hotel elevator. The Cardinals won the game in 11 innings, but Bowman had to be escorted from the park by policemen. Medwick returned to the lineup several days later, but he was never quite the same.

Q Like Joe DiMaggio, Ted Williams, and Hank Greenberg, he lost three years from the heart of his baseball career due to World War II military service. Otherwise, he would have hit considerably more than 359 home runs. Of whom do we speak?

A Johnny Mize, the "Big Cat." He spent the first six years (1936–1941) of his major league career with the Cardinals, and was then traded to the Giants and later to the Yankees, where he finally got some World Series action. Modern-day sabermetricians love Mize, who had a very high on-base percentage and is still the only man to have hit 50 home runs in a season and struck out fewer than 50 times, which he did in 1947.

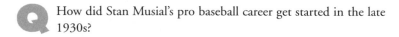

Q How did Stan Musial's pro baseball career get started in the late 1930s?

A Musial, out of Donora, Pennsylvania, was a pitcher at first. He did well in two seasons with the Cards' minor league team in West Virginia, but Rickey was thinking of releasing him due to inconsistency and bouts of wildness. While playing with a team in Florida, he got encouragement and support from his manager, Dickie Kerr, the former White Sox star. Musial, already a competent batter, was made into an outfielder. He was hitting .426 toward the end of 1941 when the Cards were convinced he was for real and brought him up.

Q The Cardinals hosted the Dodgers on May 7, 1940. Were they able to beat Leo Durocher's club?

A Yes, by a score of 18-2. There were 49 total bases on 20 hits. Thirteen went for extra bases, and seven of those were home runs—two each by Johnny Mize and Eddie Lake.

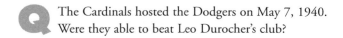

Q How many All-Star Games were held at Sportsman's Park?

A Three—1940, 1948, and 1957.

Q He won 100 games for the Cubs in the early 1930s before coming over to St. Louis. He was known as the "Arkansas Hummingbird," singing and playing guitar in the Mudcat Band, a clubhouse hillbilly combo. Name him.

A Lon Warneke, who had starred for a couple of pennant winners in Chicago. He threw a no-hitter against Cincinnati in 1941, a year before the Cubs reacquired him. As a result, Warneke missed out on the Cards reaching the Fall Classic three straight times. He served in the war effort and later got back into the game as a National League umpire.

Q The 1941 Cardinals dealt with a series of crippling injuries and fought a grueling season-long pennant race with Brooklyn, ending up 2½ games back. Rookie outfielder Stan Musial made his debut on September 17, in the heat of that pennant race. What did two of Musial's veteran teammates say about him?

A Pitcher Ernie White said, "Pressure? I don't think anyone ever explained to him what it meant. We were fighting for our lives, and this kid comes up cool as ice and starts hitting line drives that made the ball bleed." First baseman Johnny Mize echoed that: "If they would have brought Musial up earlier, we would have won the pennant in 1941."

Q Five players from the 1942 World Series champs did not play in '43 because they were off fighting the war. Name them.

A Pitcher Johnny Beazley, infielders Jimmy Brown and Frank "Creepy" Crespi, and outfielders Terry Moore and Enos Slaughter.

Q The 1942 Cards, who won 106 games en route to the NL crown, were the youngest team in the major leagues. What else is notable about them?

A Every player with the exception of pitcher Harry Gumbert had come up through the farm system put in place by Branch Rickey.

Q Max Lanier, who won 55 games (plus a couple of World Series victories) for the Cardinals from 1941 to 1944, was one of a dozen major leaguers who jumped to the Mexican League after the '46 season. What was the result of that bold move?

A Lanier and the others faced poor playing conditions and broken contract promises. After just one year south of the border, he sought to return to the Cardinals in 1948. But commissioner Happy Chandler imposed a five-year suspension on Lanier and his confederates. They filed suit in federal court, saying that baseball's reserve clause violated U.S. antitrust law—essentially the same claim made by Curt Flood 22 years later. The dispute was settled in June 1949 when Chandler lifted the suspensions and the players dropped the suit. Lanier finished his 14-year career with the Cardinals, Giants, and Browns.

Q Lanier's son, Hal, had a major league career as well. Of what did it consist?

A He was an infielder with the Giants and Yankees from 1964 to 1973 and served as a coach with the Cardinals from 1981 to 1985. Hal Lanier also managed the Astros in the late 1980s.

Q Game 1 of the 1942 World Series was played before a packed house at Sportsman's Park. The Yankees were ahead, 7-0, and Red Ruffing was working on a no-hitter in the eighth inning. Who spoiled it?

A Terry Moore, with a single. In the ninth, St. Louis scored four runs and then loaded the bases. Stan Musial came to the plate with a chance to do something big, but he ground out.

Q What rookie had two complete-game wins in the 1942 World Series?

A Johnny Beazley. This right-handed native of Nashville had gone 21-6 with a 2.13 ERA in the regular season. Soon after the Series ended, Beazley did his World War II duty. While pitching for an Army team, he severely hurt his arm. Beazley came back but tried in vain to regain the form that had carried him to such heights in 1942.

Q Name the stocky third baseman who hit a ninth-inning homer in Game 5 of the 1942 World Series to break a 2-2 tie and clinch the championship for the Cardinals.

A Whitey Kurowski, out of Reading, Pennsylvania. He overcame childhood osteomyelitis to become one of the best third basemen of the 1940s, leading the NL three times in putouts, twice in fielding average, and once each in assists and double plays. Kurowski's best year was 1947, when he batted .310, hit 27 homers, and had 104 RBIs.

Q Branch Rickey left St. Louis soon after the 1942 World Series, destined to run the show for the Brooklyn Dodgers. Was the severing of the 25-year relationship between Rickey and owner Sam Breadon amicable?

A Yes, but Breadon may have been secretly pleased about the departure of Rickey, who had drawn a large salary. With the war effort causing all belts to be tightened, that was a concern. Furthermore, Breadon may have grown weary of the constant news articles that praised Rickey's baseball acumen. In Brooklyn, Rickey put together another immensely productive farm system and helped the Dodgers win six pennants between 1947 and 1956.

Q What was the turning point of the 1943 NL pennant race?

A It happened during a game between the Cards and Dodgers at Sportsman's Park. After Brooklyn pitcher Les Webber knocked Musial down four times, catcher Walker Cooper came to the plate. After grounding out, he stepped on the foot of first baseman Augie Galan. The Dodgers' catcher, Mickey Owen, leaped on Cooper, precipitating a brawl. The Redbirds won their next 11 games en route to another pennant. Brooklyn faded to third place.

Q What three St. Louis pitchers had the best ERAs in the National League in 1943?

A Howie Pollet (1.75), Max Lanier (1.90), and Mort Cooper (2.30). The entire staff had a 2.57 ERA.

Q This Nebraskan played baseball against his father's wishes, enjoying a 13-year big league career capped by the Cards' 1926 title. In late 1929, he was handed the managerial reins and sought to impose a measure of discipline on the players, but they did not respond. Owner Sam Breadon then sent him down to the minors. Who was he?

A Billy Southworth. Despite his struggles with the bottle, he did well and was brought back up more than a decade later. The Cardinals flourished under him this time. From 1942 to 1944, Southworth presided over one of the most dominant three-year stretches in National League history, as they won 316 games, three pennants, and a pair of World Series titles. Southworth took a lucrative offer (more than three times what he had been making in St. Louis) from the Boston Braves and led them into the first division and a flag by 1948. But that team soon fell into chaos and bickering as some rebelled against his rules and regulations. It did not help that he was back in his cups. Southworth was fired midway through the 1951 season, not long before the Braves high-tailed it to Milwaukee.

Q Southworth, known also as "Billy the Kid," died in 1969, but he has not been forgotten. How so?

A Some baseball historians insist he belongs in the Hall of Fame, based not so much on his playing career—although he was a major contributor to the Cards' 1926 championship—but his record as a manager. A .642 winning percentage in St. Louis and having pulled the Boston Braves up to first in the 1948 NL race are solid credentials.

Q This native of Germantown, Illinois, signed a minor league contract with the Cards in 1942 for $75 a month. Three years later, he was the team's starting left fielder and led the NL in stolen bases. Name him.

A Red Schoendienst. He moved to second base and stayed there for the remainder of his 19-year career. With sure hands and quick reflexes, Schoendienst was with the Cards when they won the 1946 World Series. He was no weak-hitting middle infielder, either. In 1953, he batted .342, hit 15 homers, and scored 107 runs. After a trade to the Giants and another to the Braves, he helped Milwaukee win the 1957 World Series.

Q Schoendienst was back in St. Louis in 1961. In what capacity?

A He was a player-coach, getting ready for a long run as the team's manager. He held that job from 1965 to 1976, during which time the Cards won 1,041 games. The redhead served as an emergency manager in 1980 and again in 1990, and is even now a special assistant to GM Walt Jocketty.

Q What dubious distinction does Schoendienst hold?

A He was a member of three teams that lost a World Series despite jumping to a 3-1 lead: as a player with the 1958 Milwaukee Braves when they lost to the New York Yankees, as the manager of the 1968 Cardinals who lost to the Detroit Tigers, and as a bench coach on the 1985 St. Louis team that lost to the Kansas City Royals.

Q Due to wartime travel restrictions, the 1943 World Series was to be a 3-4 format, with the first three games at Yankee Stadium. Did Billy Southworth's men win any of those games before heading home?

A Just Game 2, a 4-3 victory in which shortstop Marty Marion and first baseman Ray Sanders homered.

Q Two brothers from Atherton, Missouri, were members of the Cards' World Series teams of 1942, 1943, and 1944. Name them.

A Mort and Walker Cooper. Mort was a fastballing pitcher who won 65 games for St. Louis during those three seasons, earning National League MVP honors in 1942. The starting (and losing) pitcher in the 1942 and 1943 All-Star Games, he was sent to the Braves in May 1945 after leaving the club over a salary dispute. Walker, two years younger than Mort, was a fine catcher, a 6' 3", 210-pound heavy hitter. A man given to playing practical jokes on his teammates, he was named to every NL All-Star squad from 1942 to 1950 (there was no game in 1945; anyway, he was in the Navy most of that season). In 1947, while playing with the New York Giants, he batted .305, drove in 122 runs, and hit 35 homers. Mort Cooper closed out his 18-year big league career with the Cardinals in 1957.

Q The 1944 World Series was an all-St. Louis affair, matching the NL Cardinals and the AL Browns. Since they shared Sportsman's Park, there was no travel as such. Had that ever happened before?

A Only once, in 1922 when the Giants and Yankees played at New York's Polo Grounds.

Q The Cards, clearly the best team in the major leagues, matched their 1943 record by going 105-49. They finished far ahead of Pittsburgh and their other NL competitors. How had the Browns won their pennant?

A They won 89 games and clinched it on the final day of the season, edging Detroit. The 1944 season was baseball's nadir in the 20th century, which may be why the long-moribund Browns finished atop the AL standings. The talent pool had been depleted to the point that some players had been declared 4-Fs by their draft boards—men whose physical defects precluded military service but not playing baseball. Others were virtual misfits, has-beens, and alcoholics. The situation was almost as severe the next season, when the Browns used a one-armed outfielder named Pete Gray.

Q This rookie was a starter in the regular season, with a 17-4 record. He relieved Max Lanier in the sixth inning of the final game of the 1944 World Series. Name him.

A Ted Wilks. He and Lanier wrote the final chapter to the Browns' Cinderella season, securing a second title in three years for the Cardinals.

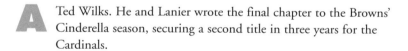

Q Name the second-string catcher who came in to pinch-hit in the 11th inning of Game 2 in the '44 Series.

A Ken O'Dea, whose single scored the decisive run. Reliever Blix Donnelly got the win.

Q At 6' 2" and 170 pounds, he disproved the theory that shortstops had to be small men and was among the best at his position throughout the 1940s. A member of the NL All-Star squad seven straight years, he hailed from Richburg, South Carolina. Identify him.

A Long-armed Marty Marion, who was nicknamed "the Octopus" for the way he snared balls hit in the infield. National League MVP in 1944, he helped St. Louis win four pennants and three championships. Marion managed the Cards, Browns, and White Sox from 1951 to 1956 but never got above third place.

Q This left-handed outfielder came from Pascagoula, Mississippi, and was known as "the Hat." Who was he?

A Harry Walker, who had four stints with St. Louis between 1940 and 1955. Unfortunately for St. Louis, his best year came in 1947 when he batted .363 with the Phillies. Walker was one of the stars of the Cardinals' 1946 World Series championship team; his double drove in the winning run in Game 7 against the Boston Red Sox. He batted .412 and had six RBIs in that Series. Walker, who hit just 10 home runs in his career, was a highly respected batting coach.

Q He was born in Morgan City, Louisiana, but was raised in Houston, where he attended Rice Institute. He pitched for the Cards in the mid-1920s and later helped run the farm system. When Billy Southworth bolted for the Boston Braves job after the 1945 season, he became St. Louis' manager. Name him.

A Eddie Dyer. He inherited a strong Cardinals club that had won three NL pennants from 1942 to 1944, and finished second in 1941 and 1945. Dyer had the challenge of blending returning war veterans and young players with those left over from the Southworth era. He was in the dugout five seasons, but the 1946 title was surely Dyer's high-water mark. With it, the Cardinals' two decades of baseball dominance came to an end as they reverted to bridesmaid status and sometimes worse.

Stan the Man.

CHAPTER THREE

THE MAD DASH

The son of a North Carolina tobacco farmer, Enos "Country" Slaughter spent 22 years in the major leagues, the first 13 coming in Cardinals red. Although he was not the only man to hustle and have a hard-nosed attitude about the game, he embodied those traits. In 1946, he played in every game (including a two-game playoff defeat of the Dodgers), batted .300, and led the league in RBIs with 130. It was Slaughter's second World Series with the Cardinals, and he would have three more with the Yankees.

The '46 World Series between the Cardinals and Red Sox, which went seven games, came down to a thrilling and unforgettable moment. More than 36,000 baseball fanatics were in full-throated roar in the eighth inning at Sportsman's Park. The score was tied at 3 when Slaughter led off with a single to center field. He stayed at first as Whitey Kurowski and Del Rice failed to get on base. As Slaughter took off in an attempt to steal second, Harry Walker lined over shortstop Johnny Pesky's head. Centerfielder Leon Culberson, who had been playing a bit deep, came in fast but bobbled the ball slightly before sending it back in to Pesky.

Slaughter flew past second and was approaching third when the ball got to Pesky, near the edge of the outfield grass. What then happened remains a matter of contention. Did Pesky hesitate and lose a precious moment? He glanced at Walker, who was approaching second. It would have been an easy out, but he did not make that throw—perhaps surprised that Slaughter was attempting to score. Third-base coach Mike Gonzalez put up the stop sign, but Slaughter was having none of it. He roared through the sign and headed home. Pesky made a quick throw to his catcher, Roy Partee, but it wasn't even close. Partee took the ball several feet in front of home plate as Slaughter was sliding across, kicking up a cloud of dirt.

The game was not won just yet. The BoSox' Rudy York and Bobby Doerr singled to start the ninth inning. But Pinky Higgins forced Doerr at second, Partee fouled out, and pinch-hitter Tom McBride hit a grounder to second baseman Red Schoendienst, whose easy underhand toss to shortstop Marty Marion ended the Series. The "Mad Dash," and all the events surrounding it, has been debated and discussed by fans ever since. Poems and songs have been written about it, and about Enos Slaughter, who hustled 270 feet that day and into baseball lore. In 1999, the Cardinals erected a statue outside Busch Stadium of Slaughter crossing home plate and capturing the World Series.

Q In 1946, the Cards drew more than a million fans—1,062,553, to be exact. What was the record before that?

A In 1928, Bill McKechnie's NL champs drew 763,615 to Sportsman's Park. Home attendance first topped two million in 1967 and three million in 1987.

Q This lefty won 21 games in the 1946 regular season, started twice in the World Series, and got no decisions. Who was he?

A Howie Pollet. He faltered for two seasons but came back in '49 with a 20-9 record, leading the NL with five shutouts. Pollet's effectiveness diminished in the early and mid-1950s as he shifted from one team to another.

Q What unusual defensive ploy did the Cards try against the Red Sox in the 1946 World Series?

A When Ted Williams came to bat, shortstop Marty Marion would shift to the right side of second base. It was called "the Williams shift."

Q The outfield fences at Sportsman's Park for the '46 Series were plastered with large ads. What did the one in right field say?

A "Cardinals, National League champs, use Lifebuoy Soap. Stops B.O."

Q He grew up in an Italian-American neighborhood in St. Louis with Yogi Berra and was signed at age 16 by Branch Rickey off the sandlots for $500. In his rookie year of 1946, he had some key hits to help the Cardinals subdue the Dodgers in the playoffs. Identify this well-known baseball funnyman.

A Joe Garagiola, who had four hits in Game 4 of the '46 World Series against the Red Sox. He later played for the Pirates, Cubs, and Giants. His broadcasting career began soon after he retired in the mid-1950s, and he and a ghostwriter combined on a best-selling book, *Baseball Is a Funny Game*. Even today, Garagiola is semi-famous for his one-liners, anecdotes, and reminiscences of life in the baseball world. Garagiola has publicly advocated against players using smokeless tobacco. Many major league teams have gotten spring-training visits from Garagiola, who shares ghastly stories about what the habit of chewin', dippin', and spittin' did to some players of his generation.

Q What left-handed pitcher won three games in the 1946 World Series?

A Harry Brecheen. This screwballer threw a four-hitter against Boston in Game 2. He also singled in the Cards' first run and had a sacrifice bunt to set up two other runs. In Game 6, Brecheen won again. On a single day's rest, he pitched two innings of relief in Game 7 for his third win. His ERA in that Series was a sterling 0.45. Two years later, Brecheen went 20-7 and led the league in ERA (2.24), strikeouts (149), and shutouts (7). His final year, 1953, was spent as a member of the St. Louis Browns. He moved with them to Baltimore the next season and coached the Orioles' pitchers for 14 years.

Q Who bought the team from Sam Breadon in 1947?

A A pair of native St. Louisans, Robert Hannegan and Fred Saigh. They swung a $4 million deal despite putting up just $60,300 in cash. Hannegan, former postmaster general and chairman of the Democratic National Committee, had saved Harry Truman's political career in 1940 (in a Senate race) and in 1944 (getting him placed on Franklin D. Roosevelt's ticket). Saigh, who bought out Hannegan in 1949, was a very successful corporate lawyer and investor who owned a lot of prime real estate in downtown St. Louis. In 1950, he convinced his fellow owners to oust commissioner Happy Chandler. Saigh led opposition because he felt Chandler had threatened the reserve clause and planned to investigate allegations of owners' gambling and ties to organized crime. Surely there is no connection, but Saigh was indicted and convicted of income tax evasion in 1953 and given a 15-month prison sentence.

Q What was the upshot of Saigh being sent to the "graybar hotel"?

A He was compelled to get out of major league baseball. On February 20, 1953, he sold the Cardinals to August Anheuser Busch, Jr. for $3.75 million. Busch pledged privately and publicly not to take the team out of St. Louis. Saigh could have gotten an extra $750,000, but keeping the team in the Gateway City was quite important. Businessmen in Milwaukee and Houston dearly wanted to buy the team and bring it to their cities.

Q Was Busch, known both as "Augie" and "Gussie," a prominent person in St. Louis?

A Born and raised in the city, he turned a small family operation into the world's largest brewing company. Busch was a master showman and irrepressible salesman. To celebrate the repeal of Prohibition in 1933, he had a brilliant idea. Recalling the draft horses that used to pull beer wagons in Germany and pre-auto-motive America, he arranged for eight of these huge equine animals to haul a case of Budweiser beer down Pennsylvania Avenue to President Franklin D. Roosevelt at the White House. Busch—technically, the Anheuser-Busch Corporation—owned the Cardinals from 1953 until his death in 1989.

Q What was Busch's first order of business after buying the club?

A He purchased Sportsman's Park from the St. Louis Browns— who were on their way to Baltimore—and renamed it for his family, although the media and fans ignored this change in stadium nomenclature to a large extent.

Q What did Busch aver shortly after becoming owner of the Cardinals?

A "My ambition is, whether hell or high water, to get a championship baseball team for St. Louis before I die."

Q Busch, who was married four times, was known for a hair-trigger temper, but he also had a zest for life. Give one example.

A Before home games in the National League playoffs and World Series home games, he sometimes rode into Busch Stadium on the Clydesdale wagon while waving a red cowboy hat.

Q What Cards pitcher has given up the most home runs in a season?

A Murry Dickson, who surrendered 39 in 1948. A native of Tracy, Missouri, Dickson was on the mound when St. Louis beat Brooklyn in the decisive Game 2 of the 1946 league playoffs. In the World Series, he started Game 7 against the BoSox as the Cardinals won another title. Dickson was traded to Pittsburgh in 1949, leading the NL in defeats three straight years. A pitcher with a vast array of deliveries, Dickson was with the Yankees when they won the 1958 World Series.

Q This Phoenix-born shortstop's playing career spanned 1949 to 1959, and he tied teammate Stan Musial for the NL lead in runs scored (105) in 1952. Identify him.

A Solly Hemus, who had his share of run-ins with umps and opponents. Hemus managed the Cardinals from 1959 until mid-way through the 1961 season as Johnny Keane was moved up.

Q Wilmer "Vinegar Bend" Mizell, a 6' 3" pitcher from Mississippi, was known for his control problems. Give three examples.

A In 1952, when he was a rookie with the Cardinals, he led the NL in walks. On September 1, 1958, he shut out Cincinnati on four hits but gave up nine walks and five stolen bases. After being traded to the Pirates in 1960, Mizell started Game 3 of the World Series, and gave up four hits and two walks before being yanked by manager Danny Murtaugh.

Q Saigh, who was worth more than $70 million when he died in 1999, was considered a generous and fair owner to players and fans alike. Give one example of each.

A In 1952, it was contract time for Stan Musial. Saigh told him to fill in the amount he felt was suitable. Musial wrote down $85,000, and Saigh thought that was fine. For the fans, he tried to make a visit to Sportsman's Park as pleasant and affordable as possible.

Q The career of this third baseman from Steubenville, Ohio, got off to a fine start. He batted .304 in 1949 and represented St. Louis in the All-Star Game, and he led the league in stolen bases the next season. Identify him.

A Eddie Kazak. Because of injuries, he soon lost his job to Tommy Glaviano. Kazak's career ended in 1952 with the Reds.

Q What did Glaviano do in a game against the Dodgers at Ebbets Field on May 18, 1950?

A He made four errors, three of them on successive plays in the ninth inning. This allowed Brooklyn to rally and win the game.

Q He signed with St. Louis in 1949 and was initially tried as a pitcher, but he hit so well that the Cardinals shifted him to third base. He labored in the minors, served in the U.S. Army for two years, and finally made the team in 1955. Name him. Hint: He would win five Gold Gloves and hit 282 home runs in a 15-year career.

A Ken Boyer. Stellar defensively from the start, he was just as good with the bat. In 1960 and '61, Boyer led the team in batting average (.304 and .329), home runs (32 and 24), and RBIs (97 and 95). His career peaked in 1964 when he was National League MVP and hit a grand slam home run in Game 4 of the World Series, giving the Cardinals a 4-3 victory. He had a single, a double, and a homer in Game 7, and scored three runs as St. Louis clinched its first title since 1946.

Q What kind of shape was the Cardinals organization in when Augie Busch made his purchase in 1953?

A In spite of the sustained excellence of Stan Musial, there had been stasis and decay due to the departure, several seasons earlier, of "The Mahatma"—Branch Rickey. More than a decade would pass before the Cards were back in the World Series.

Q Harvey Haddix went 20-9 for the 1953 Cards, but he will always be remembered for what game?

A He was pitching for the Pirates on May 26, 1959, at County Stadium against the Milwaukee Braves. Haddix retired 36 straight batters, pitching 12 perfect innings, but his Pittsburgh teammates also failed to score. In the 13th inning, Felix Mantilla reached first on Don Hoak's error (thus Haddix's shot at a perfect game was over) and went to second on a sacrifice. Haddix, tiring, intentionally walked Hank Aaron, after which Joe Adcock homered. Haddix pitched 12½ innings, threw a one-hit complete game, and still lost.

Q Who was the first black player in St. Louis Cardinals history?

A Tom Alston, a 6' 5", 210-pound first baseman with a degree from North Carolina A&T. He had played with a team in Jacksonville and another in Saskatchewan, Canada, before getting into "organized ball" in the Class C minor leagues. Alston reached the San Diego Padres of the Pacific Coast League and was there through 1953. At that time, he was sold to the St. Louis Cardinals, who gave him more seasoning with the Rochester Red Wings of the International League. He made his major league debut on April 13, 1954, in a game against the Cubs. Alston played in 66 games during his rookie season, batting .246 with 4 home runs and 34 RBIs. He committed seven errors. Not a bad start for the young man, but his showing declined drastically as he played just 25 more games over the next three seasons, sometimes going down to the Omaha Cardinals of the American Association. Alston was out of the game by 1957.

Q In what context did Tom Alston integrate the team?

A The Cardinals had featured an unmistakable Southern flair for more than two decades. The Gashouse Gang and the hillbilly music played with banjos in the team's clubhouse were but two examples. In 1947, the Cardinals—led by Enos Slaughter—were alleged to have attempted to boycott games against the Brooklyn Dodgers and their rookie second baseman, Jackie Robinson. The Indians (Larry Doby) integrated soon thereafter, then the Browns (Hank Thompson), the Giants (Monte Irvin), the Braves (Sam Jethroe), the White Sox (Minnie Miñoso), the Athletics (Bob Trice), and the Cubs (Ernie Banks) had led the way. On the same day Alston suited up at Sportsman's Park, Curt Roberts was doing the same at Forbes Field with the Pittsburgh Pirates.

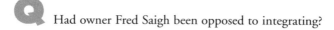 Had owner Fred Saigh been opposed to integrating?

Perhaps not, but when Augie Busch bought the team in 1953, he made it clear that the longstanding racial skittishness was absurd and had to end. He paid what seemed like a very high price ($100,000 and four players) for Alston and got him ready to come to the Gateway City. Alston, who never spoke of mistreatment by any of his teammates, developed emotional disorders and later spent time in a pair of mental institutions. He died on December 30, 1993, in Winston-Salem, North Carolina.

 Who managed the Cardinals from 1952 to 1954?

Eddie Stanky, an intense little man who annoyed opponents and umpires to no end. He had been with the Cubs, Dodgers, Braves, and Giants before landing in St. Louis toward the end of his playing days. The teams he managed never rose above third place, so "the Brat" was sent on his merry way. He managed the White Sox a decade later and also coached at the University of South Alabama.

Q Larry Jackson was a mainstay for the St. Louis pitching staff for nearly a decade, averaging well over 200 innings per year. He was traded to Chicago in October 1962. How did he do for the Cubbies in 1964?

A Jackson proved he had plenty left in the tank, going 24-11, pitching 297.2 innings, and registering 148 K's. When he was traded to the expansion Montreal Expos in 1969, Jackson declined, returned to his native Idaho, and became a sportswriter and state legislator. He served four terms in Boise and ran for governor in 1978 but was not elected.

Q Harry Walker prepped as a skipper in the Cardinals' minor league system in the early 1950s and was called up from Rochester of the International League in 1955 to replace Eddie Stanky. Was it a wise move?

A No. The Cards fell two places in the standings under Walker, losing 67 of 118 games. He was replaced, by Fred Hutchinson, at the end of the season. Managing jobs would later come in Pittsburgh (1965–1967) and Houston (1968–1972), although his teams never got into the playoffs.

Q Name the right-handed pitcher who went 15-18 with St. Louis in the early 1950s and whose younger brothers would have better and longer careers.

A Cloyd Boyer, the older brother of Ken Boyer and Clete Boyer— both superlative third basemen.

Del Rice played with the Cardinals from 1945 to 1954, before moving on to the Braves, Cubs, Orioles, and Angels. A catcher, he made up for his slowness afoot with his glove, a good arm, and an ability to handle pitchers. How many bases did Rice steal in his 17-year big league career?

Two.

He homered in his first big league at-bat and was 1954 rookie of the year (beating out Hank Aaron of Milwaukee) with the Cards, hitting .304. He was also a fine outfielder, but St. Louis dealt him in 1959. Identify this man with the lunar last name.

Arkansas native Wally Moon. He led the relocated Los Angeles Dodgers to the '59 World Series title. He was also there when "dem Bums" beat the Minnesota Twins in 1965.

In 1955, St. Louis had another rookie of the year—a slender, bespectacled center fielder who batted .281, hit 17 homers, and drove in 68 runs. Who was he?

Bill Virdon. But he started slowly in 1956, so general manager Frank "Trader" Lane sent Virdon to Pittsburgh in exchange for Bobby Del Greco and Dick Littlefield. Not a wise move. Virdon rebounded to bat a career-high .319 and was a fixture in center in the Steel City for nearly a decade. After retiring, he managed the Pirates, Yankees, Astros, and Expos, winning nearly 1,000 games.

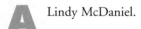 The career of this Oklahoma native began with the Cardinals in 1955 and ended with the Royals in 1975. He pitched in 987 games and won 119 in relief, and had more than 300 teammates, including Stan Musial, Ernie Banks, Willie Mays, Juan Marichal, and Mickey Mantle. Who was he?

A Lindy McDaniel.

 He played football and baseball at LSU, was the 1948 NL rookie of the year with the Boston Braves, and spent most of the 1956 and '57 seasons as the Cardinals' shortstop. Name him.

A Alvin Dark, who managed the 1974 Oakland A's to a championship.

Q Identify the man who replaced Red Schoendienst at second base for the Cardinals.

A Don Blasingame, who held down that spot for most of the late 1950s. He was a blazing base runner, particularly fast at getting down the first base line. Blasingame has the second-lowest rate of hitting into double plays in major league history. He was at his best in 1957, when he hit .271 and had career highs in home runs (8), RBIs (58), runs (101), hits (176), and stolen bases (21). He was with the Reds in 1961 when they lost to New York in the World Series.

Q This reserve shortstop of Greek descent played for the Cards twice—1954 to 1956 and 1959 to 1962. Who was he? Hint: He later managed the Milwaukee Brewers to two last-place finishes.

A Alex Grammas.

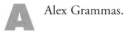

Q Who hit three inside-the-park home runs between May 30 and June 14, 1959?

A Ken Boyer. He also had a 29-game hitting streak that season.

Q St. Louis obtained this stylish, left-handed first baseman from the Giants in 1959, and he was so good with the glove that Stan Musial returned to the outfield for the remainder of his career. Identify him.

A Bill White, who hit at least 20 homers for the Cards six straight years (1961–1966). After his retirement in 1969, White served as play-by-play man for several teams and was president of the National League from 1989 to 1994.

Q He was born in Omaha and had a series of health problems during his early years, but he turned into a fine athlete—worthy of a basketball scholarship at nearby Creighton University. Who was he? Hint: He was almost certainly the finest pitcher in St. Louis Cardinals history, a man with a hellacious fastball, a darting slider, a looping curve, and pinpoint control.

A Bob Gibson, who got a $4,000 bonus to sign with the Cardinals in 1957, although he played a year with the Harlem Globetrotters before starting his pro baseball career. His first two years with the Cardinals were not especially impressive—six wins and 11 losses. But by 1962, Gibson had the first of nine 200-strikeout seasons. He would win 251 games (plus seven in the 1964, 1967, and 1968 World Series) for the Cardinals over a 17-year career.

Q Gibson, a fierce competitor, did not hesitate to throw inside and loved to show batters who was in charge. Give one example.

A In 1967, Gibson came back from having his ankle broken by Roberto Clemente's line drive up the middle. The next time Gibson faced Clemente, he sailed a fastball over the Pittsburgh star's head. For the remainder of his career, Clemente never had another hit off Gibson.

Q Was Gibson any good in 1968?

A He was the MVP of the National League, with a 22-9 record, 1.12 ERA, 268 strikeouts, and 13 shutouts. In one 92-inning span, Gibson allowed just two earned runs. He set a still-extant record in Game 1 of the World Series, striking out 17 Tigers. He was so dominant that Major League Baseball decided the batters needed some help, so the pitcher's mound was lowered by five inches.

Q Did Gibson ever throw a no-hitter?

A He did, on August 14, 1971, in a night game at Three Rivers Stadium. Gibson had plenty of offensive support from his teammates in an 11-0 victory over the Pirates.

Q Did Gibson have other baseball talents besides pitching?

A Yes. He was a fine hitter, with a lifetime .206 average; only one other pitcher since World War II has been above the .200 mark. Gibson's managers—Solly Hemus, Johnny Keane, and Red Schoendienst—sometimes used him as a pinch hitter. As if that were not enough, Gibson ran the bases well, so they even used him as a pinch runner now and then.

Q What advice did Hank Aaron give Dusty Baker before he went out to face Gibson for the first time?

A "Don't dig in against Bob Gibson, he'll knock you down. He'd knock down his own grandmother if she dared to challenge him. Don't stare at him, don't smile at him, don't talk to him. He doesn't like it. If you happen to hit a home run, don't run too slow, don't run too fast. If you happen to want to celebrate, get in the tunnel first. And if he hits you, don't charge the mound, because he's a Golden Glove boxer."

Q We know the St. Louis All-Stars were a failed pro football team back in 1923. Did Sportsman's Park ever again serve as a venue for the gridiron game?

A Yes. The Chicago Cardinals moved to St. Louis after the 1959 season and played there for six seasons, until Busch Stadium was built.

Q What St. Louis shortstop hit 43 doubles in 1963 to lead the National League?

A Dick Groat, who had just come over from Pittsburgh in a trade for pitcher Don Cardwell. He had been an all-America basketball player at Duke (and even played one season for the Fort Wayne Pistons of the NBA) and spent a decade with the Pirates. Groat won a title with the Bucs in 1960 and another with the Cards in 1964.

Q This lefty won 17 of 25 decisions for the Phillies in 1950, helping them win their second NL championship of the 20th century. He continued to pitch successfully into the late 1950s but was stricken with a sore arm and was cut. The Cards signed him, and he repaid them with six good seasons. Identify him.

A Curt Simmons, who turned himself from a hard thrower into a breaking-ball pitcher. He won 15 games in 1963 and 18 in 1964, starting two games in the World Series; in the sixth inning of Game 6, he surrendered home runs to Roger Maris and Mickey Mantle on consecutive pitches. Simmons finished up his 20-year career with the Cubs and Angels.

Q Who formed the National League's infield in the 1963 All-Star Game?

A Bill White at first base, Julian Javier at second, Dick Groat at short, and Ken Boyer at third—all Cardinals.

Bob Gibson, MVP of the 1964 and 1967 World Series.

CHAPTER FOUR

CHAMPS AGAIN

It had been a long drought—18 years, to be exact. Since 1926, the Cardinals had not gone more than seven seasons (1935–1942) between pennants. Surely there is no cause-and-effect relationship, but they did not get back to the World Series until the season after Stan Musial retired. How nice it would have been for Stan the Man to finish up his career in the Fall Classic.

The 1964 Cardinals did not have an easy path to the NL pennant. They were in eighth place in June, at which time the Cards swung a trade that brought Lou Brock over from Chicago. They were nine games behind Philadelphia in August when owner Augie Busch decided he had seen enough. He fired GM Bing Devine, and it appeared that manager Johnny Keane would be leaving soon as well. To the amazement of virtually everyone, the Cardinals went 30-14 the rest of the way. Thanks in large part to the Phillies' historic collapse, St. Louis won the pennant by one game.

Keane's Cardinals were pitted against the New York Yankees. The '64 Series would be the last hurrah for the pinstripers' dynasty of Mickey Mantle, Whitey Ford, Yogi Berra, Roger Maris, Bobby Richardson, and other such players. The Yankees would soon fall to last place, and it would be 12 years before they returned to the World Series.

There was no shortage of drama. In the ninth inning of Game 3, Mantle reached deep for that old Yankees magic, hitting Barney Schultz' knuckleball into the right field stands to win it. The very next day, Ken Boyer unloaded on Al Downing with a grand slam that provided all the runs St. Louis needed. And Tim McCarver came through with a three-run blast in the 10th inning of Game 5—this after New York had scored two in the bottom of the ninth to tie things up. Bob Gibson's third start in this Series came on two days' rest. St. Louis was ahead, 7-3, after eight innings. Gibson was tiring, but Keane preferred to have his workhorse on the mound rather than a fresh reliever. He gave up solo home runs to Mantle and Phil Lenz but held on for the victory. Soon after the Series, there was drama of a different kind as the Yankees fired Berra. He was replaced by Keane, who had just quit as the Cardinals manager.

Q How did Keane do as manager of the Yankees?

A It was a serious mismatch. New York was a team of aging stars, not inclined to listen to an outsider. Compounding Keane's misery, he replaced Yogi Berra, a true Yankee. His club came in sixth in 1965, and he was fired early in the next season.

Q Identify the Cards' starting catcher on Opening Day 1964.

A Bob Uecker, recently obtained from the Milwaukee Braves. Sound defensively but weak with the bat, Uecker later made a career out of broadcasting and baseball humor.

Q One of the worst trades the Chicago Cubs ever made took place in the middle of the 1964 season. Who was involved?

A It was basically the Cubs giving up outfielder Lou Brock in exchange for Cards pitcher Ernie Broglio. General manager Bing Devine went after Brock at the insistence of manager Johnny Keane to augment team speed and solidify the Cards' lineup, still trying to adapt after the retirement of leftfielder Stan Musial the year before. Brock averaged .348 as St. Louis drove to the pennant in the last week of the 1964 season. He then batted .300 with a home run as the Cardinals beat New York in the World Series.

Q The Cardinals signed him in 1963, despite doubts that he could throw hard enough to make it in the major leagues. Within four years, however, he was part of the starting rotation and on his way to winning 329 games—trailing only Warren Spahn among left-handers. Who was he?

A Steve Carlton, the first pitcher to win four Cy Young Awards. His 4,126 strikeouts is second only to his contemporary, Nolan Ryan. Carlton worked fanatically to develop the fastball those scouts did not think he had.

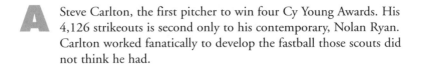

Q Carlton, who started and won the 1969 All-Star Game, could be contentious (he stopped talking to the media in 1978) and told Busch he wanted a raise. He did not get it. This scene was repeated after he went 20-9 in 1971. How exorbitant were his demands?

A Carlton sought a $10,000 raise to $65,000. Management balked, trading him to Philadelphia for Rick Wise. It was one of those trades that seem utterly foolish in retrospect. Carlton had a tremendous season in 1972, winning 27 games—almost half of the Phillies' total of 59 that year. Lefty played 24 seasons, hanging on a bit too long with the Giants, White Sox, Indians, and Twins.

Q He was a native son, born and raised in St. Louis. He played baseball and football at the University of Missouri before embarking on his big league career with the Cards. Name him. Hint: He hit a game-tying two-run homer off Whitey Ford in Game 1 of the 1964 World Series.

A Right fielder Mike Shannon. When Roger Maris was acquired in 1967, Shannon turned himself into a third baseman. His homer off Boston's Gary Bell was the key blow in Game 3 of the 1967 Series. Shannon's solo homer in the final game of the '68 Series was St. Louis' only run off Mickey Lolich as the Tigers prevailed.

Q Shannon played just 52 games in 1970 and had to retire prematurely. Why?

A He had a kidney disorder, but that did not end his connection with the Cards. Beginning in 1972, Shannon worked in the radio booth with Jack Buck, Joel Myers, Wayne Hagin, and John Rooney, and is still at it today.

Q This Memphis native hit a tiebreaking homer in the 10th inning to win Game 5 of the 1964 World Series. Two years later, he was an All-Star and was the first catcher to lead the National League in triples (13). And in 1967, he finished second to teammate Orlando Cepeda for National League MVP. Name him. Hint: He remains a prominent figure in baseball.

A Tim McCarver. He soon began a broadcasting career with the Phillies, Mets, Yankees, and Giants. McCarver has been in the booth for more than a dozen NLCS and World Series.

Q McCarver once went out to the mound to discuss matters with pitcher Bob Gibson. What was Gibson's blunt response?

A "The only thing you know about good pitching is that it's hard to hit. Now get back behind the plate." McCarver did as he was told.

Q A lot of work had been done on Sportsman's Park back in 1953, but there was only so much modernizing a facility of that vintage could take. If the Cardinals were to prosper, they would eventually need a new stadium. Busch, city officials, and civic leaders put together a major redevelopment plan for that area of downtown St. Louis. When did their efforts bear fruit?

A Ground was broken in 1964 for what would be called Civic Center Busch Memorial Stadium—mercifully shortened to Busch Stadium. The $25 million facility was designed by architect Edward Durrell Stone and had an arched design meant to echo the Gateway Arch, which was completed in 1965. It was one of a slew of circular, multipurpose stadiums (along with those in Washington, New York, Houston, Atlanta, Pittsburgh, San Diego, Cincinnati, and Philadelphia). Critics called them "cookie-cutter stadiums."

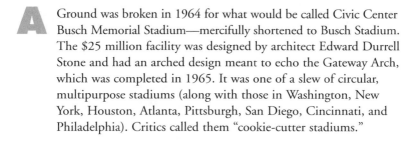

Q Were any tears shed over the razing of Sportsman's Park?

A Perhaps a few. Major league baseball had been played at that spot since 1881, where the Gashouse Gang cavorted and where Stan Musial showed his stuff. The Cardinals continued to call it home for the first month of the 1966 season before Busch Stadium opened on May 12. In that first game, the Cardinals took 12 innings to down the Atlanta Braves, 4-3.

Q What are the main changes Busch Stadium saw during its 40 years of existence?

A Artificial turf was there from 1970 to 1995, after which grass made its return. Dimensions in center field and the power alleys were altered from time to time. And when the NFL Cardinals left town in 1987, management tried to make Busch Stadium more of a "pure" baseball environment.

Q The 1966 All-Star Game was held at St. Louis' new stadium. Who won, and what made that contest so memorable?

A The NL won it, 2-1, in the 10th inning when Maury Wills of the Dodgers singled off Pete Richert of the Senators, driving in the Cardinals' Tim McCarver. The bigger story was the 105-degree heat, which had people passing out in the stands and players taking oxygen in the dugouts.

Q When Bob Gibson suffered a broken ankle in 1967, who moved into the Cardinals' starting rotation?

A Nelson Briles, a gritty control artist from California. He won nine games in a row, led the NL in winning percentage (.737, 14-4) and the Cardinals in ERA (2.43). Briles, who started two games in the World Series, won one of them as St. Louis beat Boston in seven. He won a pair while pitching for the Pirates in the '71 Series, as well.

Q Between 1962 and 1972, Gibson led the Cardinals in complete games every year—with one exception. What was it?

A In 1967, a 29-year-old rookie named Dick Hughes had 12 complete games and a 16-6 record. Hughes had arm trouble the next season, and his career was over by 1969.

Q This speedy native of the Dominican Republic started in the Pirates' farm system and was traded to the Cardinals in 1960 in return for Vinegar Bend Mizell. He soon established himself as the team's everyday second baseman for a dozen years. Who was he?

A Julian Javier, whom general manager Bing Devine compared favorably with Rogers Hornsby, Frankie Frisch, and Red Schoendienst. Javier hit .360 in the 1967 World Series against Boston, and his three-run homer in Game 7 enabled Bob Gibson to win his third Series game and bring the title to St. Louis. When his wife had a baby boy in 1964, Javier named him after his old teammate, Stan Musial. Stan Javier, who surely had baseball in his blood, played with eight major league teams over a 17-year career.

Q How was Javier honored by the people in his hometown of San Francisco de Macoris?

A The Gigantes del Cibao play their home games at Estadio Julian Javier, a 12,000-seat facility.

Q This man, born in Minnesota but raised in North Dakota, took part in more World Series games (41) in the 1960s than any other player. Who was he?

A Roger Maris. He helped the Bronx Bombers reach the Series in 1960, 1961, 1962, 1963, and 1964, and did the same with the Cardinals in 1967 and 1968. Maris, who had clouted 61 homers for New York in '61, savored his two years in St. Louis. He hit a total of 14 home runs while wearing the St. Louis uniform.

Q Lou Brock led the NL in stolen bases eight times, finishing his career in 1979 with a record 938 stolen bases (broken by Rickey Henderson 12 years later). Brock has some critics, however. What do they contend?

A Some people thought Brock did not merit enshrinement in the Hall of Fame in 1985. In spite of a good batting average and his electrifying work on the base paths, his stature is in dispute because he struck out often (1,730 times), walked seldom (761 bases on balls), and was a defensive liability for the Cubs and Cards (196 errors).

Q This Puerto Rican, known as the "Baby Bull," had been NL rookie of the year with the Giants in 1958 and was MVP with the Cardinals in 1967. Who was he, and what were his numbers?

A Orlando Cepeda, who put together a .325 batting average, hit 25 home runs, and drove in 111 runs. Unfortunately, he did not contribute much in the World Series, with just three hits in 29 at-bats. Cepeda was later convicted for participating in a drug-running operation in San Juan, which delayed his election to the Hall of Fame, but it finally happened in 1999.

Q What reserve outfielder for the 1967 champion Cards was later traded to Cincinnati, and helped get the Big Red Machine up and running?

A Bobby Tolan. His best year was 1970, when he batted .316 and stole 57 bases to lead the National League.

Q Red Schoendienst tied a World Series record in 1967 by using eight pitchers in Game 6. Name them.

A Dick Hughes, Ron Willis, Nelson Briles, Jack Lamabe, Joe Hoerner, Larry Jaster, Ray Washburn, and Hal Woodeshick.

Q What was the pitching matchup in Game 7 of the 1967 World Series?

A Gibson versus Jim Lonborg, the American League's Cy Young Award winner. Lonborg, who had already scored a pair of complete-game wins (as had Gibson), was pitching on two days rest. He struggled from the start, giving up three hits and throwing a wild pitch in the third inning. This 7-2 loss ended Boston's "Impossible Dream" season.

Q What record did Lou Brock set in the '67 Series?

A That of stolen bases. He had seven off Red Sox pitchers.

Q Having won three games in the World Series, Gibson joined a very select group. What other men had done it before?

A Just four: Babe Adams of Pittsburgh (1909), Stan Coveleski of Cleveland (1920), Harry Brecheen of St. Louis (1946), and Lew Burdette of Milwaukee (1957). Mickey Lolich of Detroit (1968) and Randy Johnson of Arizona (2001) have since won three Series games for their clubs.

Q A Michigan native, he was brutalizing minor league pitching, so the Cards brought him up in 1968. Within a couple of years, he had replaced Tim McCarver behind the plate. He stayed there until 1981 when a feud with manager Whitey Herzog sparked a trade to Milwaukee. Name him.

A Ted Simmons. Although he was not great defensively, the long-haired Simmons batted above .300 seven times, hit at least 20 homers six times, and topped 90 RBIs eight times. Simmons was faster than most catchers, recording 483 career doubles. He has Hall-of-Fame advocates, and for good reason. When compared with other catchers in Cooperstown, Simmons has very strong credentials: he scored more runs than nine of them, and none can equal his 2,472 hits.

Q This $50,000 bonus baby went 12-9 in his rookie season of 1962. A shoulder separation minimized his effectiveness the next few seasons, but he did his part in winning a title for the Cardinals in 1967. Who was he?

A Ray Washburn. He won Game 3 of the 1968 World Series against Detroit but was rocked in Game 6 as the Tigers went on to win it.

Q Washburn no-hit the San Francisco Giants, 2-0, at Candlestick Park on September 18, 1968. What gave that achievement added distinction?

A Just one day earlier, the Giants' Gaylord Perry had pitched a no-hitter of his own, beating the Cardinals and Bob Gibson. Never before in major league history had back-to-back no-hitters been thrown in the same series.

Q This native of Dubuque, Iowa, went 8-2 and had a 1.47 ERA for the 1968 Cardinals. Name him. Hint: He threw with a sidearm delivery.

A Joe Hoerner, who was used exclusively in relief during his 14-year career, which also included stops in Houston, Philadelphia, Atlanta, Kansas City, Texas, and Cincinnati. Hoerner did rather well against top competition, holding Hall of Famers Willie Mays, Bill Mazeroski, Hank Aaron, Ernie Banks, Tony Perez, Reggie Jackson, Willie Stargell, and Carl Yastrzemski to a collective .101 batting average (9-for-89).

Q Who sang the national anthem before Game 5 of the '68 World Series? Hint: He is best known for a remake of the Doors' classic, "Light My Fire."

A José Feliciano.

Q The Cardinals might have expected to win the 1968 Series, given that the Tigers' pitching star was largely ineffective. Who was he?

A Denny McLain, who won 31 games in the regular season. He lost Games 1 and 4 but got a victory in Game 6, a 13-1 runaway.

Q What happened in the fifth inning of Game 5 of the '68 Series that dimmed the Cards' hopes?

A Lou Brock was on second base when Julian Javier singled. Speedy player that he was, Brock tried to score. But he came in standing up rather than sliding. Detroit catcher Bill Freehan easily tagged him out, and a rally was snuffed just like that.

This center fielder had just won his sixth straight Gold Glove when he misjudged a fly ball by the Tigers' Jim Northrup with two out in the seventh inning of Game 7 of the 1968 World Series. No one knows for sure, but the Cardinals might have won their third title of the decade if not for his critical defensive mistake. Name him.

 Curt Flood.

 Flood played more than 1,800 games in a 15-year career, but what is his most lasting legacy?

 His challenge of baseball's longstanding reserve clause, which kept players beholden for life to the teams holding their contracts. Flood was part of a multi-player deal with Philadelphia in 1969, but he refused to report to the lowly Phillies. He filed a $4.1 million lawsuit and sat out the 1970 season. The case, Flood v. Kuhn (407 U.S. 258), went all the way to the Supreme Court. Although the justices ruled against him, Flood found vindication five years later when an arbitrator ruled that since Orioles pitchers Dave McNally and Andy Messersmith played for one season without a contract, they were free agents. This decision in effect dismantled the reserve clause, opening the door to widespread free agency and much bigger contracts for major league baseball players.

Q He was born just across the Mississippi River in Granite City, Illinois, earned a degree in electrical engineering from Washington University, and was the Cards' primary shortstop between 1966 and 1971. Identify him.

A Dal Maxvill. He may have been a smooth fielder, but he was notoriously weak at the plate, hitting six home runs in a 14-year career. In the 1968 World Series, Maxvill had 22 at-bats and did not get a single hit. However, on April 14, 1969, against the Montreal Expos, he hit a grand slam—the first ever in major league play in Canada. Maxvill served as St. Louis' general manager from 1985 to 1994, during which time the Cards won two pennants.

Q Steve Carlton struck out 19 Mets on September 15, 1969. Did he win the game?

A No, he did not. Ron Swoboda hit two home runs, and New York took a 4-3 victory.

Q This Brooklynite broke into the majors at age 19 in 1960 with the Milwaukee Braves as a catcher but also filled in at first and third. A five-time All-Star at the hot spot (and a Gold Glove winner in 1965), he was traded to St. Louis in a straight-up swap for Orlando Cepeda. Identify him.

A Joe Torre. He was at his best in 1971, leading the National League in batting average (.363), RBIs (137), hits (230), and total bases (352). For that offensive production, Torre was named the league's MVP. He was shipped to the Mets after the 1974 season for Tommy Moore and Ray Sadecki.

Q What did Torre do in his post-playing days?

A Early in the 1977 season, Mets manager Joe Frazier was canned. Torre, then hanging on as a third baseman, was offered the job. Although he tried briefly to be a player-manager, he soon saw the difficulty if not folly of such an attempt and gave up playing, closing his 18-year career. He managed the Mets for five years but never had a winning record. He then took over as the Atlanta Braves' skipper, leading them to one National League West title in three years. After six years in the broadcast booth, he was back with the Cardinals. His teams won 351 and lost 354, and never got into the playoffs. He was sent packing in the middle of the 1995 season. A few months later, the New York media was up in arms over the news that George Steinbrenner had chosen Torre as the Yankees' manager. They changed their tune when he immediately guided them to the Fall Classic for the first time since 1981. Championships in 1998, 1999, and 2000 gave Torre unprecedented stature. In August 2007, he passed Casey Stengel as the Yanks' all-time winningest manager. He became manager of the Los Angeles Dodgers the next season.

Q He hit two homers for the Boston Red Sox against St. Louis in the 1967 World Series. This strong-armed outfielder played for the Cards in 1974 and 1975, batting over .300 both years. Identify him.

A Reggie Smith, who was traded to the Dodgers in the middle of the 1976 season.

Q What center fielder was named 1974 NL rookie of the year, batting .309 with 81 runs and 30 stolen bases?

A Arnold "Bake" McBride, who would top .300 seven times in his career. He was with the Phillies when they won the 1980 World Series and finished up doing part-time duty with the Indians.

Q On July 17, 1974, Bob Gibson registered the 3,000th strikeout of his career. Who went down?

A Cesar Geronimo of the Cincinnati Reds.

Q The date was September 10, 1974. Lou Brock stole his 105th base of the season, breaking the record held by Maury Wills of the Los Angeles Dodgers. Against whom did Brock get this theft?

A The opponent was the Philadelphia Phillies, and the battery mates were pitcher Dick Ruthven and catcher Bob Boone.

Q Identify the "Mad Hungarian."

A Al Hrabosky, a chunky southpaw reliever with a smoking fastball, whose career peaked with the Cardinals in 1975 as he went 13-3, had a 1.67 ERA, and 22 saves. Hrabosky, with his Fu Manchu and flowing black hair, would stomp around the mound to psyche himself up between pitches. He later played for the Royals and Braves, and has been a Cardinals announcer for many a moon.

Q This 6' 6" pitcher, who had been with the Braves for most of a decade, went 9-8 with the 1975 Cardinals. He did not stay in St. Louis long, moving on to the Phillies the following year. Name him.

A Ron Reed, who played basketball at Notre Dame and with the Detroit Pistons of the NBA. He averaged 9.4 points and 6.4 rebounds per game in two seasons (1966 and 1967) with the Pistons.

Q In 1976, this 23-year-old Arizona native had a 2.52 ERA, best in the National League. Who was he?

A John Denny. He was even better in 1983 while playing for the Phillies. Denny went 19-6 with a 2.37 ERA to win the Cy Young Award. He also won Game 1 of the World Series against the Baltimore Orioles, the only victory for Paul Owens' club.

Q Who set a team record for most home runs by a catcher in 1977?

A Ted Simmons, with 21. He would break his own record the next year by hitting 22 dingers.

Q What happened in franchise history on August 29, 1977?

A In a game against the Padres, Lou Brock stole his 893rd base, breaking Ty Cobb's career mark.

Q He was a native of St. Louis, signing a Cardinals contract straight out of high school in 1946. He never rose above the AAA level, partly because service during the Korean War hindered his development. But his success managing the Denver Bears caught the attention of Cards management, and he was brought up in 1977. Who was he, and how successful was he?

A Vern Rapp is the man in question. It was not easy replacing the popular Red Schoendienst, but his Cards improved by 11 games and finished in third. The players, unaccustomed to his old-school ways, did not favor Rapp and he was out after 17 games of the 1978 campaign. Rapp coached in Montreal for five years and then got another managing job—with the Cincinnati Reds in 1984. He was on thin ice from the start and was soon ousted.

Q Who took Rapp's place in the St. Louis dugout?

A Coach Jack Krol succeeded him on an interim basis, but former Cardinals star Ken Boyer was ticketed for the permanent job. Despite being all but idolized from within and without the organization, Boyer did not last much longer than Rapp had.

Q Bob Forsch threw a no-hitter against the Phillies at home on April 16, 1978. When was the last time a Cards pitcher had a no-no in St. Louis?

A Fifty-four years earlier, Jesse Haines threw one against the Boston Braves at Sportsman's Park.

Q The Cardinals traded pitcher Eric Rasmussen to the Padres in May 1978. Who did they get in return?

A Right fielder George Hendrick, a player with a nice, fluid style. He was in St. Louis through 1984, blossomed into a .300 hitter, and twice drove in more than 100 runs. "Silent George," for reasons known only to him, refused to speak to the media, but teammates and fans liked him.

Q Ted Simmons hit a game-tying home run off the Cubs' Bruce Sutter in May 1978. He had circled the bases and was coming toward home plate. What happened next?

A Simmons was jawing with umpire Paul Runge about the latter's questionable ball-and-strike calls. Runge waited for Simmons to touch home plate and then tossed him from the game.

Q What pitcher gave up the 3,000th hit of Lou Brock's career on August 13, 1979?

A Dennis Lamp of the Cubs.

Q What reserve first baseman had an 11th-inning pinch-hit grand slam to beat the Astros at Busch Stadium in 1979?

A Roger Freed.

Q The best-fielding first baseman in the majors for most of his 17-year career, he won 11 straight Gold Gloves. In 1979, he batted .344 and shared National League MVP honors with Willie Stargell of Pittsburgh. Identify him.

A Keith Hernandez, who was known as a carefree, fun-loving player. He was traded to the last-place Mets for a journeyman relief pitcher in 1983 amid manager Whitey Herzog's allegations that he had been snorting cocaine—allegations that were later proven to be true. In New York, Hernandez lived down his old reputation. He was a key player on the team that won the 1986 NL pennant and beat Boston in the World Series.

Q This switch-hitting shortstop was known around the St. Louis clubhouse as "Jump Steady." He was also known for swinging at first pitches and bad pitches. Just about any pitch at all would do, as he struck out 1,092 times in a 16-year career. Identify him.

A Garry Templeton, who led the league in 1979 with 211 hits and 19 triples.

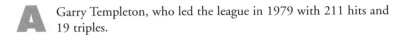

Q Templeton was not chosen as the NL's starting shortstop in the 1978 All-Star Game, despite having better numbers than either Dave Concepcion of Cincinnati or Larry Bowa of Philadelphia. Upon learning he was merely a reserve, what was Templeton's famous response?

A "If I ain't startin', I ain't departin'!" In a 1981 incident, Templeton was heckled by fans and responded with an obscene gesture. This resulted in a fine, suspension, and trade to San Diego. In return, the Cards got an Ozzie Smith who was fast coming into his own. Templeton, however, did well for the Padres, leading them to a National League pennant in 1984.

Q This bearded relief pitcher, a Pennsylvania native, was with the Cubs for five years, winning the 1979 Cy Young Award. He joined the Cardinals in 1981. The next year, he earned a save in the pennant-clinching victory over Atlanta in the NL championship series. Who was he?

A Bruce Sutter, one of the first pitchers to master the split-fingered fastball. He saved two games in the 1982 World Series and was on the mound at the end, striking out Gorman Thomas of the Milwaukee Brewers. Sutter saved 300 games in his 12-year career and reached the Hall of Fame in 2006, his 13th year of eligibility. Some baseball purists were not happy about that because Sutter pitched in just over 1,000 innings and had a losing record (68-71).

Q What 1981 trade reaped big dividends for the Cardinals?

A They sent pitcher Bob Sykes to the Yankees for a free-swinging minor league outfielder named Willie McGee. As a rookie the next year, McGee batted .296 and swiped 24 bags, coming in third in rookie-of-the-year voting as the Cards beat the Brewers in the World Series. McGee was part of the foundation of a St. Louis team that would reach the World Series again in 1985 and 1987.

Q What pitcher led St. Louis in strikeouts each season from 1978 to 1980? Hint: He stood 6' 4", wore a bushy moustache, and was known for fidgeting, pacing, and wild gesticulations on the mound.

A Pete Vuckovich, who had played earlier with the White Sox and Blue Jays. Vuckovich would win the 1982 AL Cy Young Award while pitching for Milwaukee. He met and fell to his ex-teammates in that year's World Series.

Q Augie Busch generally adhered to a policy of noninterference, both for a corporation that now has annual sales of $10 billion and for his baseball team. But not always. Give one example.

A In 1982, he led a movement among major league owners to dump commissioner Bowie Kuhn.

Q What man, who described himself as "one tough Dominican," had a 1.35 ERA, and won Games 3 and 7 of the 1982 World Series?

A Joaquin Andujar. He had worked mostly out of the bullpen with the Astros for six years before joining the Cards in the early 1980s. He won a total of 41 games in 1984 and '85, helping St. Louis to another pennant in the latter season. Andujar pitched miserably in the last two months and was hit hard in the post-season—by the Dodgers in the NLCS and by the Royals in the World Series. He lost Game 3 and had a disastrous relief showing in Game 7. Sent into the game by manager Whitey Herzog in the fifth inning when the Cards were already losing badly, Andujar gave up a hit and a walk, and began complaining so vociferously about the umpiring that he was sent to the showers.

Q Identify the "Wizard of Oz"—the baseball player, not the 1939 film classic starring Judy Garland.

A That's Ozzie Smith, who was born in Alabama but raised in Los Angeles. The winner of 13 Gold Gloves and widely recognized as one of the best defensive players of all time, he spent four seasons with the San Diego Padres before the Cards acquired him in a trade. With Smith at shortstop, St. Louis promptly won the 1982 World Series over Milwaukee. The team was back in the Fall Classic three years later after Smith hit a game-winning home run against the Dodgers in the NLCS. Smith, who batted over .300 just once in his 19-year career, stole 580 bases and won a lot of games with his glove.

Q Fans remember the effervescent Smith for his range and defensive work in the field. But what else?

A The ritual backflip he performed before opening days, All-Star Games, and postseason games. After retiring in 1996, Smith kept an arms-length relationship with the franchise because of lingering bitterness over how manager Tony La Russa cut his playing time at the end and groomed Royce Clayton to take his place.

Q He was born and raised in Chicago, had a great rookie year with the Phillies, and joined the Cards in 1982. Identify him.

A Lonnie Smith, a catalyst for the 1982 champion Cardinals when he led them in hits, doubles, triples, batting average, runs, and stolen bases. In one game that season against San Francisco, he stole five bases. Smith's main weakness was erratic defensive play in the outfield. He had some drug problems but overcame them and was with the Royals when they met the Cardinals in the 1985 World Series. Smith contributed a .333 average, 4 RBIs, 5 runs, and a pair of stolen bases as KC won it. He later put on some muscle and became a power hitter in Atlanta.

Q Third-string catchers are usually pretty slow, and Glenn Brummer was no different. What rare thing did he do on August 22, 1982?

A Brummer stole home with two outs in the 12th inning to give St. Louis a 5-4 victory over the San Francisco Giants.

Q What Philadelphia pitcher beat the Cardinals, 6-2, on September 23, 1982, marking his 300th victory?

A Steve Carlton, who had been traded to the Phillies 10 years earlier.

Q By what means did the Cardinals and Brewers end up facing each other in the 1982 World Series?

A St. Louis won the National League East by three games over the Phillies and then beat the Braves, 3-0, in the NLCS. The Brewers won the American League East by one game over the Orioles. They then beat the California Angels in five games in the ALCS. Sportswriters, always looking for a witty hook, chose to call it the "Suds Series" since both cities are known for producing brewskis.

Q St. Louis catcher Darrell Porter was named MVP of the Series, but a couple of Milwaukee players had strong credentials, too. Who were they?

A Pitcher Mike Caldwell, who won two games, and third baseman Paul Molitor, who banged out five hits in Game 1 and four in Game 5.

Q Rookie Willie McGee put on a nice show in Game 3 of that Series. What did he do?

A McGee, who had just four homers all season, hit two into the cheap seats at County Stadium. He also caught a 400-foot shot off the bat of Paul Molitor in the first inning and robbed Gorman Thomas of a home run in the ninth with a leaping snag at the fence.

Q Name the St. Louis designated hitter who had two doubles and a triple in Game 6 of the '82 World Series.

A Dane Iorg, who would be the Cards' nemesis three years later as a member of the Kansas City Royals.

Q The catchers in that Series had extra motivation to win. Who were they?

A Milwaukee's Ted Simmons had spent more than a decade with the Cardinals, and St. Louis' Darrell Porter played with the Brewers from 1971 to 1976.

Q What did Porter do in later years?

A He played with the Cards through the 1985 season, spent two years with Texas, and retired after 17 seasons. Porter, one of the first pro athletes to acknowledge his problems with alcohol and drugs, cleaned up and fell off the wagon several times. He died at age 50 on August 5, 2002. The autopsy attributed his death to the toxic effects of cocaine.

Q Herzog gave the ball to a rookie pitcher and told him to win Game 6 of the 1982 Series. Identify him.

A John Stuper, who did just that. He gave up four hits and one run en route to a crucial victory.

Q The Cardinals and Brewers, managed by Harvey Kuehn, certainly had contrasting styles entering that Series. What was the main one?

A Milwaukee (known as "Harvey's Wallbangers") had hit 216 home runs in the regular season, as compared with just 67 by St. Louis.

Q What amusing incident took place during Bob Forsch's 1983 no-hitter against the Expos?

A He and Gary Carter were not exactly best buds. Forsch had promised to drill Montreal's catcher when he first came up to bat—and he did, before resuming his no-hitter.

Q He had played baseball and football at Florida A&M. In 1983, with Macon of the South Atlantic League, he set an all-time pro record by stealing 145 bases. Two years later, it was more of the same in the majors as he swiped 110, batted .267, and was named National League rookie of the year. Identify him.

A Vince Coleman. He did not stop there, leading the NL in steals every year from 1985 to 1990. Coleman, who left the Cards by free agency and played for the Mets, Royals, Mariners, Reds, and Tigers, finished with 752—sixth most in the history of the game.

Q What freak accident kept Coleman from participating in the 1985 World Series?

A Before the fourth game of the NLCS against the Dodgers, Coleman was doing stretching exercises when the automatic tarpaulin at Busch Stadium rolled over his leg. The Cardinals managed to win that game and the series, but they eventually fell to the Royals in the World Series.

Q Coleman had stolen successfully 50 straight times until a game with the Expos on July 28, 1989. What catcher threw him out?

A Nelson Santovenia.

Q Mike Jorgensen parlayed modest offensive skills into a 17-year career with the Mets, Expos, A's, Rangers, Braves, and Cardinals. But he was a fine first baseman with a team-first attitude. What did he do in St. Louis?

A Jorgensen played for the Cards in 1984 and '85, mostly as a left-handed pinch hitter and late-game defensive replacement. He did not contribute much to the team reaching the 1985 Series, but he paid his dues and was chosen to replace Joe Torre when St. Louis' 1995 season got off to a bad start. A 42-54 record was not enough to keep him around, however.

Q This switch-hitting LA native made it to the bigs with St. Louis in 1984, displaced Ken Oberkfell and Andy Van Slyke, and was the team's primary third baseman for the next seven years. Identify him.

A Terry Pendleton. Manager Whitey Herzog loved his great range, lightning reflexes, rifle arm, and base-path savvy. Pendleton also became a powerful hitter as the years went on. The Cards reached the World Series with him twice, but he was traded to Atlanta after the 1990 season. He proceeded to win the National League MVP award and propel the Braves to a pennant.

Q Willie McGee hit a lot of line-drive singles that turned into doubles because of his blistering speed and the deep dimensions of Busch Stadium. What was McGee's best year with the bat?

A In 1985, he led the NL in batting (.353; the highest in history for a switch-hitter), hits (216), and triples (18). McGee, who later played for Oakland, San Francisco, and Boston, finished up back in St. Louis as a part-timer. He retired in 1999 with a .295 lifetime batting average in tow.

Q This versatile player, who spent two years with the Mets before joining the Cardinals in 1985, holds the team record for most games in a season—163 in 1989. Identify him. Hint: He is a native of Puerto Rico. Another hint: He is now St. Louis' third base coach.

A José Oquendo.

Q What Cardinals left-handed pitcher has the best winning percentage in a season?

A John Tudor, whose 10-2 record in 1987 comes to .833. He also had an impressive season in 1985, although it started out rather badly. Tudor had gone 1-7 through May and was giving up runs like nobody's business. Then he turned it around by winning 20 of his next 21 decisions and lowering his ERA to 1.93. Tudor had 10 shutouts, a record that may never be approached, given the increased use of five-man rotations and managers' tendency to bring in relievers at the drop of a hat.

Q How did Tudor do in the 1985 postseason?

A His pitching propelled the Cardinals into the playoffs. Although he lost Game 1 of the NLCS to the Los Angeles Dodgers, he won Game 4 to even it up as St. Louis went on to win the series, 4-2. The World Series began with Tudor on the mound against the Kansas City Royals. He won Games 1 and 4 but imploded in the third inning of Game 7 as KC rolled to an 11-0 victory and the title. An enraged Tudor threw a post-game tantrum, punching an electrical fan and cutting his pitching hand.

Q Who replaced the injured Vince Coleman in the 1985 postseason?

A Tito Landrum, who batted .429 against Los Angeles in the NLCS and .360 against Kansas City in the World Series. Landrum, who was flawless in the outfield, had a strong case for MVP honors.

Q This injury-prone outfielder-turned-first baseman spent a decade with the Giants and never reached the postseason. With a trade to St. Louis in 1985, that changed. Who was he?

A Jack "the Ripper" Clark, a superb clutch hitter. He won Game 6 of the 1985 NLCS against the Dodgers with a ninth-inning homer off Tom Niedenfuer. Clark, a menacing man with a bat in his hands, was never better than in 1987 when he batted .286, hit 35 homers, and drove in 106 runs. An ankle injury in September may have cost him the MVP and—far more important—kept the Cardinals from beating the Twins in the World Series. After a contract squabble, Clark signed as a free agent with the Yankees. He retired in 1992, shortly after declaring bankruptcy due to some "expensive hobbies," as his attorney put it. Those hobbies included a $717,000 Ferrari and numerous other fine automobiles.

Q The Cards, facing Kansas City in the '85 Fall Classic, were going for their 10th championship. They had won 10 more games in the regular season than their cross-state counterparts. Did Dick Howser's Royals have a chance?

A After they lost the first two at home, things were looking bad for KC. But the Royals' ace, Bret Saberhagen, righted the ship with a 6-1 victory in Game 3. John Tudor had a complete-game shutout in Game 4, putting St. Louis on the verge of a champagne celebration in the locker room of Busch Stadium.

Q Game 6 of the "Show-Me Series" was not a happy one for fans of the Redbirds. What happened?

A It was a pitchers' duel between the Cards' Danny Cox and the Royals' Charlie Leibrandt. They put up goose eggs until the eighth inning, when Terry Pendleton scored. But the bottom of the ninth would feature controversy and a collapse by Herzog's team. Jorge Orta led off with a routine grounder to Jack Clark, who tossed the ball to pitcher Todd Worrell for what appeared to be an out. Close but definitely out. Nevertheless, umpire Don Denkinger erroneously ruled him safe. Orta was later forced out at third, but a KC rally was on. Darrell Porter had a passed ball. Then, with the bases loaded and one out, ex-Cardinal Dane Iorg looped a single to right field that drove in two runs. Herzog and his players fumed afterward, blaming Denkinger for his missed call and the loss.

Q Who was the home plate umpire the next night at Royals Stadium?

A Don Denkinger, and the Cardinals knew it. Saberhagen, Series MVP, threw a five-hit complete game, and the Royals scored two in the second inning, three in the third, and six in the fifth as they roared to the 1985 championship.

Q How bad was St. Louis' offense in that World Series?

A The Cards batted an anemic .185 and scored just 13 runs—both all-time lows for a seven-game Series. The worst offenders were Andy Van Slyke (1-for-11), Ozzie Smith (2-for-23), and Tom Herr (4-for-26).

Q Two Cardinals batters share the dubious record of most strike-outs—five—in a game. Name them.

A Dick Allen did it against the Phillies on May 24, 1970, and Ray Lankford against the Cubs on August 8, 1998.

Q The Cardinals and Giants have had their share of bad blood over the years, including the time José Oquendo and Ozzie Smith, taking offense at how San Fran's Will Clark had broken up a double play, did a little tag-team on him. Name another instance.

A In a 1986 game, St. Louis was up by eight runs when Vince Coleman stole second and third. Managers Whitey Herzog and Roger Craig nearly came to blows, while some of their players did—just a bunch of highly fortified alpha males at each other's throats.

Q Reserve first baseman Mike Laga did something unique on September 15, 1986. What was it?

A The Cards, pennant-winners the year before, were near the end of a forgettable season when they faced the Mets at home. Laga, who was not an especially powerful hitter, nevertheless got a hold of one. The ball rocketed up and completely out of Busch Stadium, two-thirds of the way down the right-field line. The ball was foul, and it supposedly landed in a flowerbed across the street from the stadium.

Q Despite playing in 39 games in 1990, he was a rookie the next year when he took over the centerfield spot from Willie McGee. He led the NL with 15 triples, and stole 44 bases, scored 83 runs, and once hit for the cycle. Name this native of Modesto, California.

A Ray Lankford, who played 11 seasons in St. Louis before finishing up with San Diego.

Q What did Lankford do on Opening Day 1994?

A The season started with a bang as Lankford hit a leadoff home run against the Reds. St. Louis went on to win, 6-4.

Q How did Herzog get his team back into the playoffs in 1987?

A The Cardinals went 95-77 in the regular season, beat the Giants in seven in the NLCS, and were expected to make quick work of the Minnesota Twins in the World Series.

Q When did the Cards realize they might be in for a fight?

A In Game 1, when a raucous crowd in Minneapolis did more than observe the Twins' 10-1 victory. The fans' noise (later revealed to have been electronically enhanced) reverberated off the white roof of the Metrodome, unnerving the NL champs. Frank Viola was the winner, and Joe Magrane was the loser for St. Louis.

Q The Cards tied it up in Game 4. Who was the hero that night?

A Tom Lawless, who had gone 2-for-25 in the regular season. He hit a three-run homer in the fourth inning, more than enough offense for St. Louis to win.

Q The Twins won Game 6 of the '87 Series due to a couple of big boppers—Kirby Puckett and Kent Hrbek. Did the Cards win the deciding game?

A No. Viola and closer Jeff Reardon brought down the curtain on St. Louis in a 4-2 win. There were a couple of questionable calls by the umpires, but those things tend to even out.

Q Who caught for St. Louis in the late 1980s and managed the Royals from 2002 to early 2005?

A Tony Pena, a native of Monte Cristi in the Dominican Republic. He is now a coach with the Yankees.

Q What was the biggest regular season crowd ever at Busch Stadium?

A On July 20, 1994, the Cardinals and Cubs played before 53,415 fans, although the teams were tied for fourth in the NL East.

Q The Phillies and Cards were playing on April 21, 1991. St. Louis had erased a five-run deficit, tied it in the bottom of the ninth, and headed into extra innings. What was this game's explosive conclusion?

A In the bottom of the 10th, Ray Lankford was determined to score from second base on a teammate's hit, but catcher Darren Daulton was waiting at the plate in firm possession of the ball. Lankford steamrolled Daulton, delivering a brutal forearm to the chest. The ball came loose as Lankford stomped on home plate for the winning run.

Q Where were the Cardinals in the NL Central standings when a players' strike ended the 1994 season?

A They were in third place, 13 games behind Cincinnati. The team, with a record of 53-61, had a payroll of $29.6 million. The World Series, which had been played every fall for nine decades regardless of depressions, wars, and earthquakes, was canceled due to a labor dispute. The strike extended into the 1995 season, which was shortened to 144 games.

Q Attendance at major league baseball games fell off 15 to 20 percent in 1995. Did things pick up in St. Louis?

A Cardinals fans grumbled about the strike like everybody else, but they were back by 1996—almost 2.7 million. With Tony La Russa working the dugout, the club won the NL Central after once being nine games below .500.

Q Augie Busch died in 1989, but Anheuser-Busch retained ownership for another six years. Who bought the club after the 1995 season?

A A group headed by William O. DeWitt, Jr., put together $150 million to buy the franchise (valued today at $370 million), Busch Stadium, and related assets. DeWitt was born in St. Louis and has degrees from Yale and Harvard. He founded an investment firm, and one of his business ventures, the Spectrum 7 oil company, bought future President George W. Bush's Arbusto Energy, and in turn merged with Harken Energy in 1986. DeWitt connected Bush with Eddie Chiles, owner of the Texas Rangers, and Bush became nominal owner of the club. Charges of insider trading were made in some of these business transactions, but the U.S. Securities and Exchange Commission declined to prosecute Bush.

Q Does DeWitt have a baseball background?

A Yes, he does. His father, William O. DeWitt, Sr., was a protégé of Branch Rickey. He sold soda pop at Sportsman's Park and later became the team's treasurer before taking a front-office job with the rival St. Louis Browns, where he rose to general manager and majority owner. DeWitt was in charge of the Browns when they faced the Cards in the 1944 World Series. He also served as an executive with the Yankees and Tigers. By 1960, DeWitt had become GM of the Cincinnati Reds, making a number of moves that led to the 1961 National League pennant. It was not long before he bought the team from the Crosley estate. He sold it in 1966 and served as chairman of the Chicago White Sox under the flamboyant Bill Veeck in the late 1970s. One may assume that DeWitt the younger has learned a few things from his dad.

Q Did the Cards make any noise in the 1996 playoffs?

A A little. They swept the Padres in three games in the NLDS and took a 3-1 lead over the Braves—World Series champs in '95— before losing three straight.

Q Drafted by the Cardinals in 1995, he reached the majors two years later and was at the top of his game in 2001 when he went 22-7 with the use of a 95-mph fastball, a sinking two-seamer, a biting curve, and a straight changeup. Who is this native of Middletown, New York?

A Matt Morris, now a member of the Pittsburgh Pirates.

Q He grew up in Minneapolis and graduated from the University of Minnesota. He spent 13 years with Oakland and one with Colorado before coming to the Cardinals. Name him.
Hint: He is not a player.

A Walt Jocketty, St. Louis' general manager since 1995.

Q The Cardinals got a new manager in 1996. Who was he?

A Tony La Russa, a native of Tampa, Florida. He was a promising middle infielder in the early 1960s, but a shoulder injury in his rookie year never fully healed. He played a total of 132 major league games with the A's, Braves, and Cubs. His numbers were modest: .199 batting average, 7 RBIs, and 15 runs scored. La Russa earned a law degree from Florida State before Chicago tabbed him in '79. He was named American League manager of the year in 1983, when his club won the AL West, but he was fired after a slow start in 1986. La Russa had 10 years with the A's and recently finished his 12th season in St. Louis. Only the second manager to win championships in both leagues, he currently trails just Connie Mack and John McGraw on the all-time managerial wins list.

Q Who did La Russa invite to join the Cards in 1996 and '97?

A Dennis Eckersley, who had been a truly great reliever for a long time—primarily with the Oakland A's. His best was far behind him when he put on a St. Louis uni, as is seen in his stats. In 1996, Eckersley had 30 saves but a record of 0-6. The next year, he had 36 saves and went 1-5. The Cards paid him $2.2 million in the first year and $1.6 million in the second.

Q Only one native of Delaware has ever hit for the cycle in a major league baseball game. This man did it while playing for the Cards against the Rockies on May 18, 1996. Identify him.

A Utility player John Mabry.

Mark McGwire. In his 16-year career,
he hit a home run every 10.6 at-bats—
the best ratio in baseball history
(Babe Ruth is second at 11.8).

CHAPTER FIVE

THE CASE OF
THE BULKED-UP
FIRST BASEMAN

Mark McGwire hit the major leagues in 1987 with a bang. As a rookie, his stats consisted of 49 long balls, 118 RBIs, and a .289 average, so McGwire's selection as AL rookie of the year was all but certain. As it happened, another big-hitting Oakland player—José Canseco—had won the award one year earlier. McGwire played first base and Canseco was out in right, although neither was especially adept on defense. The so-called Bash Brothers were the centerpiece of an intimidating lineup that powered the A's to three straight American League pennants and a World Series title in 1989.

McGwire did not keep up that torrid pace over the next few years, partly due to back and foot injuries. But he batted .312 and had what was then a career-best 52 home run total in 1996, his last year in Oakland. The impoverished A's soon traded McGwire to St. Louis, reuniting him with manager Tony La Russa. After adjusting to NL parks and pitchers, he finished that season with 58 home runs, the most by a right-handed batter since Jimmie Foxx and Hank Greenberg. The St. Louis fans adored McGwire, and he seemed to revel in the atmosphere of the baseball-mad city, soon signing a contract extension.

In 1998, he and Chicago Cubs outfielder Sammy Sosa engaged in a suspenseful, although good-natured, attack on Roger Maris' single-season home run record of 61. In the midst of a media spectacle far exceeding what Maris had endured 37 years earlier in his pursuit of Babe Ruth's mark, McGwire was up to the task. At Busch Stadium on September 8, he hit number 62 and set off a big celebration. McGwire finished the season with an unfathomable 70 home runs—a record broken just three years later by Barry Bonds—whereas Sosa had 66.

He sent 65 more over the wall in 1999. Age and injuries caught up to Big Mac, who retired in 2001, having hit 583 home runs. It was not all wine and roses in his later years, however. McGwire had gone from carrying 215 pounds on his 6' 5" frame as a rookie to 250, and was almost a caricature of a stiff, one-dimensional player. He couldn't play defense, he struck out often, and he couldn't run the bases to save his life. It is indicative that he hit just six triples in 6,187 career at-bats. All McGwire did was stand in the box and swing. Since 1998, it had been public knowledge that he took androstenedione, an over-the-counter muscle enhancement product that had been banned by the NFL and the International Olympic Committee.

Canseco, his former teammate, published a book in 2005 entitled *Juiced: Wild Times, Rampant 'Roids, Smash Hits, and How Baseball Got Big.* In it, he categorically claimed to have introduced McGwire to steroids in 1988. Soon thereafter, McGwire, Canseco, Sosa, and two other current players were called before the House Government Reform Committee to discuss the issue. McGwire declined to answer questions under oath and stubbornly stuck to one line: "I'm not here to talk about the past." It was a public relations disaster for McGwire, who appeared to have a lot to hide. When he became eligible for Cooperstown the next year, he got just 23 percent of the vote from baseball writers who had once held him in the highest esteem.

Q The big McGwire–Sosa home run derby of 1998 has come to be seen as somewhat bogus due to the widespread suspicion that both men—and many other big league players—were doping. Who took notice?

A San Francisco Giants outfielder Barry Bonds. A pair of *San Francisco Chronicle* reporters tied him to the notorious company known as the Bay Area Laboratory Co-Operative. They alleged that BALCO provided Bonds with a wide array of performance-enhancing drugs over the next five seasons that turned him into a home-run hitting machine unlike any other. As mentioned earlier, he busted 73 in 2001, but Bonds eclipsed a more hallowed mark six years later when he broke Hank Aaron's career home run record.

Q What Florida Marlins pitcher did Mark McGwire victimize on May 16, 1998, with a prodigious 545-foot clout?

A Livan Hernandez.

Q Name the versatile batter whose 13-year career (1990–2002) was evenly divided among the Expos, Dodgers, Cardinals, Orioles, and Cubs. Hint: Montreal traded him straight up to Los Angeles in exchange for a skinny pitching prospect named Pedro Martinez.

A Second baseman Delino DeShields.

Q What Expos pitchers gave up McGwire's 69th and 70th home runs on September 27, 1998?

A Mike Thurman and Carl Pavano.

Q Edgar Renteria, the Cards' rangy shortstop from 1999 to 2004, is best known for something he did while with another team. What was it?

A With the Florida Marlins, Renteria came to the plate in Game 7 of the 1997 World Series with the score tied at 2 in the bottom of the 11th inning. He lined a single up the middle off Cleveland's Charles Nagy, driving in the winning run and making the Marlins champs of the baseball world.

Q This tough-as-nails second baseman had a 12-year career that included time with the Mariners, Mets, Brewers, Cardinals (2000–2003), and Tigers. Who is he? Hint: He is now a baseball broadcaster for ESPN.

A Fernando Viña.

Q What was the salary gap for the 2000 Cardinals?

A On the high end, first baseman Mark McGwire earned $9.3 million, while third baseman Fernando Tatis and catcher Mike Matheny both pulled down $750,000. Among the starting pitchers, Darryl Kile made $7.4 million and rookie Rick Ankiel made $202,000.

Q The Cardinals finished fourth in the NL Central in 1997, third in 1998, and fourth in 1999. Did they rise up from that mediocrity in the first year of the new millennium?

A Indeed they did. St. Louis went 95-67, drew a franchise-record 3,336,493 fans, and proceeded to the league division championship series with the Braves. They swept Atlanta in three games. But it was a different story against the Mets in the NLCS. Short-handed without the injured Mark McGwire, Mike Matheny, and Garrett Stephenson, the Cardinals fell in five.

Q This right fielder had a record-setting career at Florida State and, upon being drafted by the Phillies, he refused to sign for anything less than $10 million. He was with the Cardinals from 1998 to 2003 and had some good years, but there were injuries, and problems with fans and fellow players. Identify him.

A J.D. Drew. He left St. Louis after his agent wangled a five-year, $55 million contract with the Los Angeles Dodgers, one that included an escape clause after the second year. Drew did exercise that clause, forgoing $33 million over the next three seasons to become a free agent. He then got a $70 million deal from the Red Sox, adding fuel to charges that he is the poster boy for greedy baseball players.

Q Where did the career of outfielder Jim Edmonds begin?

A This man with the gorgeous left-handed stroke played with the California Angels from 1993 to 1999 before the Cards got him in a trade for second baseman Adam Kennedy and pitcher Kent Bottenfield. The winner of eight Gold Gloves (so far), he patrols center field with flair, providing a steady diet of spectacular catches. Edmonds' laid-back personality has sometimes made fans and teammates think he does not try hard enough. He also tends to whiff a lot.

Q What was one of Edmonds' more memorable grabs in center field?

A In a game against the Reds on July 16, 2004, Jason LaRue hit a deep shot to center field that appeared to have "home run" written all over it. But Edmonds took off running, scaled the wall, and extended his glove over it—just far enough to catch the ball, sending a disappointed LaRue back to the dugout.

Q How did Edmonds do in the 2004 NLCS against Houston?

A His extra-inning home run won Game 6, and in Game 7 he made a sparkling defensive play in center that helped St. Louis win the pennant. Two years later, Edmonds had four RBIs in the World Series for the winning Cards.

Q Name the splendid Cincinnati Reds outfielder who hit the 500th homer of his career off the Cards' Matt Morris on June 20, 2004.

A Ken Griffey, Jr.

Q What team record does Steve Kline hold?

A This right-handed reliever took part in 89 games in 2001. Kline, who played for the Cards from 2001 to 2004, is now with the San Francisco Giants.

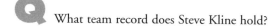

Q He was born in the Dominican Republic but moved to the U.S. at age 16. One year of junior college ball was enough to convince the Cards to draft him in 1999—but they waited until the 13th round. After a bit of minor league seasoning, he strode into St. Louis' 2001 spring training and muscled his way onto the team and the starting lineup. Name him.

A Albert Pujols, who quickly embarked upon a phenomenal rookie campaign: .329 batting average, 37 home runs, and 130 RBIs. Pujols could play third and first base or in the outfield, although he soon settled at first. His batting drew raves from all quarters. By season's end, Pujols was hands-down the NL rookie of the year and even drew MVP talk as St. Louis entered the playoffs. The Cardinals lost in the first round, but it was clear they had found a great young player.

Q Who was the last St. Louis rookie before Pujols to be selected to play in the All-Star Game?

A Pitcher Luis Arroyo in 1955.

Q Did Pujols sustain that level of excellence?

A He was National League batting champion in 2003 (.359), MVP in 2005, and a key member of the World Series champs in 2006. Pujols was the first major league player to hit 30 or more home runs in each of his first six seasons—now extended to seven—and the youngest to hit 250 home runs. Not since Ted Williams has a player begun his career with six straight 100-RBI seasons.

Q What memorable blow did Pujols strike in Game 5 of the 2005 NLCS against the Astros, down in Houston?

A With two outs in the top of the ninth, and David Eckstein and Jim Edmonds on base, Pujols took Astros pitcher Brad Lidge deep. His three-run homer was the deciding factor in the game, as the Cardinals ended up winning, 5-4. The series returned to St. Louis, although the Astros won it.

Q To what ex-Yankees great has Pujols been compared? Hint: He was a centerfielder, not a first baseman.

A Joe DiMaggio. Like Joltin' Joe, Pujols is a guy who can inflict a lot of damage with his bat while minimizing strikeouts.

Q Who made an appearance at Busch Stadium on the night of September 17, 2001?

A The Cardinals' retired announcer, Jack Buck. Baseball was resuming after the terrorist attacks six days earlier, and Buck was there to recite a poem he had written, entitled "For America." Suffering from lung cancer, sciatica, vertigo, diabetes, and Parkinson's disease, he looked rather frail and struggled to maintain his composure. It was a stirring moment for those in attendance. Buck died nine months later at the age of 77.

Q Buck, who also broadcast basketball, football, bowling, and hockey, was noted for his effortless style behind the microphone. Which of his offspring has carried on in this field?

A Joe Buck. He was raised in St. Louis, got a degree from Indiana University, and was soon doing play-by-play for the Louisville Redbirds (a minor league affiliate of the Cardinals). Then he moved up to doing Cardinals games on local television. He has since become a familiar voice nationally, doing the Super Bowl, NLDS, NLCS, and World Series.

Q The 2001 Cards matched the Astros with a 93-69 record and got into the playoffs as a wild card team. Who did they face?

A The Arizona Diamondbacks. Woody Williams and Bud Smith followed up their strong September efforts with victories in the second and fourth games, but it was not enough. St. Louis was out, and the Snakes went on to win the World Series.

Q Who replaced Mark McGwire at first base for the Cardinals in 2002?

A Tino Martinez, fresh off four World Series titles with the Yankees. He did not stay long—just two seasons—and was off to Tampa Bay and back to New York before retiring.

Q Cards pitcher Darryl Kile was found dead in his Chicago hotel room on June 22, 2002, a victim of coronary disease. Of what did his baseball career consist?

A The California native was a front-line pitcher with the Houston Astros for seven years, throwing a no-hitter in 1993. He had an arsenal of sinking fastballs and knee-buckling curves, so Colorado signed him to a big-money deal in 1998. But pitching in Denver's thin air was not easy, and his ERA ballooned. The Cards got him in 1999, and Kile proceeded to recapture much of his former glory. He won 20 games in 2000 and 16 in 2001 as St. Louis won the NL wild card. Kile's tragic death ended a career made up of 133 wins and 119 losses.

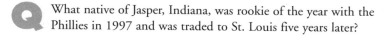

Q What native of Jasper, Indiana, was rookie of the year with the Phillies in 1997 and was traded to St. Louis five years later?

A Third baseman Scott Rolen. His best year at the plate was in 2004. In spite of injuries in the last part of the season, he had a career-high .314 batting average, 34 homers, and 124 RBIs. Although he did not play especially well in the 2006 NLDS (against San Diego) or in the NLCS (against New York), Rolen was superb against Detroit in the World Series, batting .421 with one home run and three doubles. He laced an opposite-field single in the seventh inning of Game 5 to drive in the final run in the Cards' clinching victory of that Series.

Q For what is Rolen best known?

A His defensive prowess. At 6' 4", he is tall for a third baseman, but he has won seven Gold Gloves and drawn comparisons to Hall of Famer Brooks Robinson.

Q How many men took the mound for the St. Louis Cardinals in 2002?

A A club-record 26, and they put together an ERA of 3.70.

Q With 97 victories, the Cards won the 2002 division title. They met the Diamondbacks in the first round of the playoffs. Did St. Louis avenge what Arizona had done a year earlier?

A Yes, in a three-game sweep of the World Series champs. But La Russa's offense struggled—going 3-for-39 with runners in scoring position—against the San Francisco Giants in the NLCS. They lost in a five-game series.

Q What mark did Tony La Russa set on September 10, 2003?

A When his Cards beat Colorado, he became the eighth manager in major league history to win 2,000 games.

Q This right-handed pitcher, a University of Houston alumnus, came over from the Padres in 2001 in a swap for Ray Lankford. Name him.

A Woody Williams, who took part in the 2003 All-Star Game and started Game 1 of the 2004 World Series. Since 2007, he has applied his baseball skills for the Houston Astros.

Q He was a walk-on at the University of Florida but ended up being a two-time all-SEC shortstop. Even more improbable, he was on a major league roster (with the Anaheim Angels) on Opening Day in 2001. Identify him.

A David Eckstein, a key player for the 2002 World Series champs. He joined the Cardinals three years later as a free agent. An All-Star in 2005 and 2006, he was named the '06 World Series MVP. Eckstein went 8-for-22 with 4 RBIs and scored three runs against the Detroit Tigers, and hit three doubles in Game 4.

Q What did Eckstein do against the Braves on August 7, 2005?

A In the ninth inning, St. Louis was down, 3-1. The bases were loaded when Eckstein came to bat, and he proceeded to hit it out. The last Cardinal to hit a walk-off grand slam was Tommy Herr, who did it in extra innings against the Mets on April 18, 1987.

Q What right-handed pitcher won 20 games for St. Louis in 2002 and '03, suffered shoulder problems, and was cut soon thereafter?

A Jason Simontacchi, now a member of the Washington Nationals.

Q Who threw out the ceremonial first pitch in the Cards' 2004 home opener with the Brewers?

A President George W. Bush.

Q La Russa's 2004 Cards had the best record in the major leagues, winning 105 games. Did the NL Central champs have any trouble with Los Angeles in the opening round of the playoffs?

A Not really. They cruised to a couple of 8-3 victories at Busch Stadium, but lost Game 3—the Dodgers' first postseason victory since 1988. The Cardinals reclaimed control of the series the next night at Chavez Ravine. Pujols' three-run homer in the fourth was all they needed in a 6-2 win.

Q The Cardinals moved on to face the wild-card Astros, who had finished 13 games behind them in the regular season, in the NLCS. Which team prevailed in that seven-game series?

A St. Louis took the first two games and Houston the next three. In an exciting Game 6, St. Louis was ahead by one run in the top of the ninth before Jeff Bagwell singled, driving in the tying run. The Astros' dancing turned to mourning as Jim Edmonds hit a walk-off homer in the bottom of the 12th, sending the series to a Game 7 showdown. In it, Jeff Suppan outdueled Roger Clemens, and the Cards had won their first NL pennant in 17 years.

Q The 100th World Series featured the Cardinals and what American League team?

A The Boston Red Sox, fresh off an amazing comeback against the New York Yankees. The first game was on October 23, and the last was on October 27. All four were Red Sox victories, as the Curse of the Bambino was finally put to rest. Other than some solid hitting by Larry Walker, Albert Pujols, and Edgar Renteria, the Cards had nothing. La Russa, interviewed after Game 4, was almost apologetic about the performance of his team.

Q What Cardinals radio broadcaster got in some hot water in early 2005, and what was the issue?

A Wayne Hagin. He stated or at least implied that Colorado Rockies first baseman Todd Helton was on "the juice." Helton took umbrage, and Hagin's bosses went to unusual lengths to apologize. He was out of a job not long after that.

Q What pitcher spent six years in Toronto, joined the Cards in 2003, dealt with a series of shoulder problems, and won the Cy Young Award in '05?

A New Hampshire native Chris Carpenter. In 2005, he posted a 21-5 record, had a 2.83 ERA, and struck out 213 batters. He was 2-0 in the postseason against the San Diego Padres and Houston Astros. Carpenter was on the All-Star team that season and again in 2006. He beat the Tigers in Game 3 of the World Series, soon signing a $65 million extension with St. Louis. But his shoulder problems resurfaced, and he missed most of the 2007 season. Team doctors say Carpenter may not be back at full strength until late '08.

Q With whom is Carpenter sometimes confused?

A Cris Carpenter, a right-handed reliever with the Cards from 1988 to 1992. He won 27 games in his career, which also included stints with the Marlins, Rangers, and Brewers.

Q He played college ball at Michigan State, was on the fast track to the major leagues, and anchored a powerful pitching rotation in Oakland, along with Barry Zito and Tim Hudson, before joining the Cards in 2005. Name this tall southpaw.

A Mark Mulder. On May 23, 2005, he threw a 10-inning shutout of the Houston Astros. The last National League pitcher to have an extra-inning shutout was Greg Maddux of the Cubs in 1988. Mulder's future is cloudy due to serious problems with his shoulder.

Q At 100-62, the 2005 Cardinals were again the class of the National League. Who did they sweep in the first round of the playoffs?

A The San Diego Padres. The winning pitchers were Chris Carpenter, Mark Mulder, and Matt Morris.

Q Who has been the president of the St. Louis Cardinals since 1994?

A Mark Lamping, a graduate of Rockhurst University in Kansas City.

Q It was La Russa's Cards against Phil Garner's Astros in the 2005 NLCS. Did Houston avenge its 2004 postseason loss to St. Louis?

A Yes, in six games. The most dramatic moment of the series may have come in Game 5. The Astros were one strike away from advancing to the World Series for the first time. But David Eckstein singled, Jim Edmonds walked, and Albert Pujols hit a towering three-run homer off Brad Lidge. St. Louis won, 5-4.

Q What pitcher gave Houston seven strong innings in Game 6 to win that series?

A Roy Oswalt, who won MVP honors. That, by the way, was the final game in old Busch Stadium.

Q Who announced his retirement after the Cards fell to the Astros in the 2005 NLCS?

A Right fielder Larry Walker, one of the best Canadian-born players in baseball history. His career, which began in 1989 with the Montreal Expos, included five All-Star selections, seven Gold Gloves, and one National League MVP award.

Q What happened in St. Louis at 3:07 p.m., Central Standard Time, on November 7, 2005?

A Demolition of Busch Stadium began. It took a month by wrecking ball rather than implosion, due to the nearby presence of the new stadium.

Even in a new stadium,
the historic legacy of the Cards lives on.

CHAPTER SIX

NEW HOME
ON THE BANKS OF
THE MISSISSIPPI

The Cardinals' new owners, led by Bill DeWitt, began to lobby for a new ballpark in downtown St. Louis in 1995. But progress to acquire funding was slow and tortuous. In June 2001, the Missouri State Legislature approved a new stadium, but a bill to fund it was struck down. The saga went on as DeWitt sought a location near Madison, Illinois. That, of course, got the immediate attention of St. Louis' mayor, city council, county government, and business leaders.

After much negotiation and arm-twisting, a financing plan was cobbled together for the new stadium, which was to be adjacent to the old one. The money came from private bonds, from bank loans, from a long-term loan from the county, and even a little from the team owners. Ground was broken in January 2004 for the stadium, designed by HOK Sport and built by Hunt Construction. It cost an estimated $365 million. Promises were made about the stadium rejuvenating that area of downtown, but similar promises were made four decades earlier, and they surely hadn't been fulfilled. The Cardinals announced plans for a "Ballpark Village" beyond center-field, complete with a franchise hall of fame, restaurants, shops, offices, an aquarium, residential units, and parking areas; as of early 2008, however, construction on the project hadn't begun.

The new park would also be called Busch Stadium. The terms of a 20-year naming rights deal were not released, but Anheuser-Busch was to have exclusive alcohol beverage sponsorship of all of the team's radio and TV broadcasts, promotions, use of the famous bird-on-a-bat logo, and stadium signage. Busch Stadium would have a seating capacity of 43,975, plus about 3,000 standing-room tickets. Construction was not complete by Opening Day 2006; in fact, finishing touches continued throughout that first season. The old stadium was nothing if not fully enclosed, with high walls all around. The new one, by contrast, was designed to have an open-air feel, with an unobstructed view of St. Louis' skyline and the nearby Gateway Arch. Busch Stadium has virtually the same field dimensions (336' in left, 390' in left-center, 400' in center, 390' in right-center, and 335' in right) as its predecessor, albeit with less foul territory. It favors neither hitters nor pitchers, lefties nor righties.

Amid much pomp and circumstance, the stadium opened on April 10, 2006. The ceremonial first pitches were from Albert Pujols to Willie McGee and Chris Carpenter to Bob Gibson. As is only fitting, the Cardinals won, beating the Milwaukee Brewers, 6-4.

 What streets surround Busch Stadium?

 Clark Street is on the north, Broadway is on the east, Poplar Street is on the south, and Eighth Street is on the west.

Is it true that the Cardinals milked every last dollar they could from old Busch Stadium by holding auctions for items as mundane as urinals?

Yes.

Q Which Cardinals have been named NL rookie of the year?

A Wally Moon in 1954, Bill Virdon in 1955, Bake McBride in 1974, Vince Coleman in 1985, Todd Worrell in 1986, and Albert Pujols in 2001.

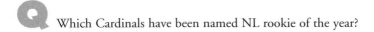

Q *Sports Illustrated* has chosen two St. Louis players as its sportsman of the year. Name them.

A Stan Musial in 1957 and Mark McGwire (along with Sammy Sosa of the Cubs) in 1998.

Q Which Cards have been named National League MVP?

A Frankie Frisch (1931), Dizzy Dean (1934), Joe Medwick (1937), Mort Cooper (1942), Stan Musial (1943, 1946, and 1948), Marty Marion (1944), Ken Boyer (1964), Orlando Cepeda (1967), Bob Gibson (1968), Joe Torre (1971), Keith Hernandez (1979, shared with Willie Stargell of Pittsburgh), Willie McGee (1985), and Albert Pujols (2005).

Q Name the Cardinals who have been enshrined in the Hall of Fame.

A Grover Cleveland Alexander, Walter Alston, Jake Beckley, Jim Bottomley, Roger Bresnahan, Lou Brock, Mordecai Brown, Jesse Burkett, Steve Carlton, Orlando Cepeda, Roger Connor, Dizzy Dean, Leo Durocher, Dennis Eckersley, Frankie Frisch, Pud Galvin, Bob Gibson, Burleigh Grimes, Chick Hafey, Jesse Haines, Rogers Hornsby, Miller Huggins, Rabbit Maranville, Bill McKechnie, John McGraw, Joe Medwick, Johnny Mize, Stan Musial, Kid Nichols, Branch Rickey, Wilbert Robinson, Red Schoendienst, Enos Slaughter, Ozzie Smith, Bruce Sutter, Dazzy Vance, Bobby Wallace, Hoyt Wilhelm, Vic Willis, and Cy Young.

Q The Cardinals have retired 10 numbers. What are they, and who are the honorees?

A 1 (Ozzie Smith), 2 (Red Schoendienst), 6 (Stan Musial), 9 (Enos Slaughter), 14 (Ken Boyer), 17 (Dizzy Dean), 20 (Lou Brock), 42 (Bruce Sutter and Jackie Robinson [his number is retired throughout the major leagues]), 45 (Bob Gibson), and 85 (for owner Augie Busch on his 85th birthday).

Q Who has the best World Series batting average in team history?

A Pepper Martin (.418), Lou Brock (.391), Julian Javier (.346), Tim McCarver (.311), and Walker Cooper (.300).

Q Which Cards have played in the most World Series games?

A Jim Bottomley and Frankie Frisch are tied at 24, followed by Chick Hafey, Whitey Kurowski, Marty Marion, and Stan Musial at 23.

Q What Cards pitchers have thrown the most innings in the World Series?

A Bob Gibson (81), Mort Cooper (45), Bill Hallahan (39.2), Burleigh Grimes (34.2), and Harry Brecheen (32.2).

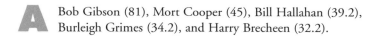

Q Name the five men who have the most hits in a St. Louis uniform.

A Stan Musial (3,630), Lou Brock (2,713), Rogers Hornsby (2,711), Enos Slaughter (2,064), and Red Schoendienst (1,980).

Q What St. Louis pitchers have thrown no-hitters, and who were their victims?

A Jesse Haines (against Boston on July 17, 1924), Paul Dean (against Brooklyn on September 21, 1934), Lon Warneke (against Cincinnati on August 30, 1941), Ray Washburn (against San Francisco on September 18, 1968), Bob Gibson (against Pittsburgh on August 14, 1971), Bob Forsch (against Philadelphia on April 16, 1978 and against Montreal on September 26, 1983), José Jimenez (against Arizona on June 25, 1999), and Bud Smith (against San Diego on September 30, 2001).

Q What St. Louis pitchers have had at least 10 shutouts in a season?

A Bob Gibson (13 in 1968), Mort Cooper (10 in 1942), and John Tudor (10 in 1985).

Q What Cardinals have had the longest hitting streaks?

A Rogers Hornsby (33 in 1922), Stan Musial (30 in 1950), Albert Pujols (30 in 2003), Harry Walker (29 in 1943), Ken Boyer (29 in 1959), Joe Medwick (28 in 1935), Red Schoendienst (28 in 1954), Lou Brock (26 in 1971), and Joe McEwing (25 in 1999).

Q What Cards have hit home runs in the All-Star Game?

A Frankie Frisch (at Comiskey Park in 1933 and the Polo Grounds in 1934), Joe Medwick (at the Polo Grounds in 1934), Stan Musial (at Sportsman's Park in 1948, Ebbets Field in 1949, Briggs Stadium in 1951, County Stadium in 1955, Griffith Stadium in 1956, and Yankee Stadium in 1960), Red Schoendienst (at Comiskey Park in 1950), Ken Boyer (at Yankee Stadium in 1960 and Shea Stadium in 1964), and Reggie Smith (at Three Rivers Stadium in 1974).

Q Who are the leaders in the number of games played in a Cardinals uniform?

A Stan Musial (3,026), Lou Brock (2,289), Ozzie Smith (1,990), Enos Slaughter (1,820), and Red Schoendienst (1,795).

Q Five Cardinals have hit more than 100 triples. Who are they?

A Stan Musial (177), Rogers Hornsby (143), Enos Slaughter (135), Lou Brock (121), and Jim Bottomley (119).

Q Name the Cardinals who have hit for the cycle.

A Cliff Heathcote in 1918, Jim Bottomley in 1927, Chick Hafey in 1930, Pepper Martin in 1933, Joe Medwick in 1935, Johnny Mize in 1940, Stan Musial in 1949, Bill White in 1960, Ken Boyer in 1961 and 1964, Joe Torre in 1973, Lou Brock in 1975, Willie McGee in 1984, Ray Lankford in 1991, John Mabry in 1996, and Mark Grudzielanek in 2005.

Q Which Cardinals have hit three home runs in a game?

A Frank Shugart in 1894, George Harper in 1928, George Watkins in 1931, Johnny Mize in 1938 (twice) and 1940 (twice), Stan Musial in 1954 and 1962, Bill White in 1961, Reggie Smith in 1976, Mark Whiten in 1993, Mark McGwire in 1998 (twice) and 2000, and Albert Pujols in 2004 and 2006 (twice). It should be noted that Whiten hit four bombs against the Reds on September 7, 1993.

Q Name the Cardinals who have hit a home run in their first big league at-bat.

A Eddie Morgan (against Chicago on April 14, 1936), Wally Moon (against Chicago on April 13, 1954), Keith McDonald (against Cincinnati on July 4, 2000), Chris Richard (against Minnesota on July 17, 2000), Gene Stechschulte (against Arizona on April 17, 2001), Hector Luna (against Milwaukee on April 8, 2004), and Adam Wainwright (against San Francisco on May 24, 2006).

Q Six Cards have gotten six hits in a single game. Who are they?

A Duff Cooley (against Boston on September 30, 1893), Roger Connor (against New York on June 1, 1895), Dick Harley (against Pittsburgh on June 24, 1897), Jim Bottomley (against Brooklyn on September 16, 1924 and against Pittsburgh on August 5, 1931), and Terry Moore (against Boston on September 5, 1935).

Q This left-handed pitcher out of Florida was good enough to merit a $2.5 million signing bonus, breezed through the minors, and was on the Cardinals' staff by 2000 at age 21. Identify him.

A Rick Ankiel, who posted an 11-7 record and had a 3.50 ERA (ninth in the league) with 194 K's. Equipped with a 95-mph fastball, a heavy sinker with lots of movement, and a devastating 12-to-6 curve, he dominated hitters, striking out almost 10 per nine innings and coming in second in rookie-of-the-year voting.

Q Ankiel obviously had a bright future as a pitcher, right?

A So it appeared, but he experienced a sudden and shocking downfall that began in Game 1 of the 2000 NLDS against Atlanta. In the third inning of that game, Ankiel's control deserted him as he allowed four runs on two hits, walking four and throwing five wild pitches before being pulled by manager Tony La Russa. Ankiel, the first pitcher to throw five wild pitches in an inning in 110 years, shrugged it off. He was back on the mound in Game 2 of the NLCS against the Mets, and it was more of the same— 20 pitches, five of which sailed past catcher Eli Marrero. The Cardinals had him checked for mechanical problems, but there were none. They were also quite careful with his psyche, but things got even worse when he was sent to the minors; in one instance, he pitched 4.1 innings, walked 17 batters, and threw 12 wild pitches.

Q After trying valiantly to regain his control, Ankiel announced in 2005 that he was converting himself into an outfielder. Was he successful in this endeavor?

A He was, both as a right fielder and at the plate. He proved himself with the AAA Memphis Redbirds and was back in "the show" by August 2007. In Ankiel's first game back, he hit a three-run homer to help the Cards beat the Padres. The St. Louis fans, knowing of his struggles, gave Ankiel a prolonged standing ovation. He even got them on the road. Ankiel kept banging out home runs at an improbable rate. The feel-good story lasted barely a month before the *New York Daily News* reported that he had received eight shipments of human growth hormone in 2004 from a pharmacy in Florida. Although HGH was not banned by Major League Baseball until '05, suspicions about Ankiel's amazing comeback continue to linger.

Q St. Louis was not the powerhouse of the previous two years in 2006, winning just 83 games. Was it enough to reach the postseason?

A Barely. The Cardinals, who finished 1½ games ahead of the Astros, met San Diego in the NLDS and won it in four. The Padres went 2-for-32 with runners in scoring position, so they had their chances.

Q Identify the MVP of the 2006 NL championship series against the heavily favored New York Mets.

A Jeff Suppan, who pitched in Games 3 and 7, compiling a 0.60 ERA. He also had a home run in the first of those games for the eventual World Series champs. After the season, Suppan signed a $42 million contract with the Milwaukee Brewers.

Q What catcher hit a two-run homer in the ninth inning of Game 7 of that series to send the Cards back to the World Series?

A Yadier Molina, who hit it off the Mets' Aaron Heilman.

Q The 2006 World Series was a rubber match of sorts. How so?

A The Cardinals had beaten the Tigers in 1934, and Detroit took revenge in 1968.

Q What controversy erupted in Game 2 at Comerica Park?

A Pitcher Kenny Rogers was found to have pine tar on his pitching hand. The umps had him wash it off, and he stayed out there for eight innings of a 3-1 Detroit win.

Q Who was called upon to get the final three outs against the Tigers, ensuring St. Louis' first championship in 24 years?

A Adam Wainwright. He got Magglio Ordoñez to ground out, gave up a double to Sean Casey, got Ivan Rodriguez to hit him a weak roller, walked Placido Polanco, and struck out Brandon Inge on a curveball.

Q St. Louis won the 2006 World Series in its brand-new stadium. When was the last time a team won the Series at home in a new stadium?

A In 1923, when Yankee Stadium opened and Miller Huggins' team beat the Giants in the Series.

Q What 5' 8" second baseman had been with the White Sox and Rockies before joining the Cards just in time to win the 2006 World Series?

A Aaron Miles. The following year, on August 4, 2007, manager Tony LaRussa had thrown in the towel in what would be a 12-1 loss to the Washington Nationals. Miles, who had not pitched in a game since he was 14, was called on to handle the eighth inning. He got all three batters out.

Q By beating the Tigers in the 2006 Series, La Russa became just the second manager to have won titles in both leagues. Name the other.

A Sparky Anderson, who did it with Cincinnati and Detroit.

Q This right-handed pitcher, a native of Mississippi, played for the Red Sox, Phillies, Reds, and Cardinals in a six-year career that ended with his death on April 29, 2007. Identify him.

A Josh Hancock, who was killed when the car he was driving struck the rear of a tow truck that was there to move a vehicle from a prior accident. The police report revealed that at the time of the collision, Hancock was intoxicated with a blood-alcohol level of 0.157, almost twice the legal limit in Missouri. Hancock, who was not wearing a seatbelt, was texting on his cell phone when the accident occurred. Just three days earlier, he had been involved in another drunken driving accident.

Q What are the St. Louis Cardinals' minor league teams?

A The Memphis Redbirds of the Pacific Coast League, the Springfield Cardinals of the Texas League, the Palm Beach Cardinals of the Florida State League, the Quad City Swing of the Midwest League, the Batavia Muckdogs of the New York-Penn League, and the Johnson City Cardinals of the Appalachian League.

Q Where do the Cardinals hold spring training?

A Roger Dean Stadium in Jupiter, Florida. The stadium, which was built in 1998, has room for 7,800 fans. It is shared by St. Louis and the Florida Marlins during Grapefruit League play. When the big boys are gone, it is home for the Jupiter Hammerheads and Palm Beach Cardinals of the Florida State League.

Q For whom is the press box at Busch Stadium named?

A Bob Broeg and Rick Hummel, both of whom are part of the writers' wing of the Baseball Hall of Fame. The naming took place in 2007.

Q The 2007 season was not a happy or satisfying one for La Russa as his team failed to repeat—or even contend for—another championship. What happened?

A It began with his own arrest for drunken driving in spring training, the death of Josh Hancock, and the investigation of pitcher-turned-hitting star Rick Ankiel for using HGH. La Russa gave interviews indicating that the players had ceased listening to him and that "strained relationships" within the organization might soon bring his tenure to an end.